8-15

In "Raising Righteous and Rowdy Girls," Doug Giles reinforces the notion that little women don't need to be pampered by their fathers to turn out right. And having met his beautiful daughters, I know his philosophy works. As a strong-willed woman who thinks her daddy is the greatest guy in the world, I can tell you this is a must-read for every man who hopes to earn the same title.

— S.E. Cupp
Best Selling Author & Fox News Analyst —

If I ever have daughters I'm going to raise them up like Doug Giles has done: strong, proudly feminine, tough as nails, Proverbs 31 girls. "Raising Righteous and Rowdy Girls" is an excellent guide which shows how a father can raise up real women in a society that desperately needs them.

— Dana Loesch, Editor BigJournalism.com,
Talk Radio Host, Television Commentator. —

Doug Giles' approach to raising girls is the most effective method I have ever seen. He promotes the perfect balance between spirituality, intelligence, physical prowess and good health; all of which combined creates successful and happy women. I have known Hannah and Regis for over 10 years, and they stand as a shinning testament to the lessons presented in this book.

— Pedro Valente
Head Professor at Valente Brothers Jiu-Jitsu —

I made Doug Giles' book on raising girls required reading for my four sons. Talk about a masterpiece for raising true American women in the spirit of God, country, and family Giles' book is hard-hitting, spoken in straight talk, and interesting from cover to cover. No matter what gender your child is, READ THIS BOOK!

— Kevin Jackson Best Selling Author,
The Big Black Lie, —

The feminist movement morphed into a man-hating cult leaving young women bereft of the skills to either be ladies or gentlemen ... until Doug Giles stepped in with this marvelous book to show how he raised his daughters to be well-rounded, accomplished ladies of action. This is a must read how-to guide.

—Frank Miniter,
Bestselling Author of "The Ultimate Man's Survival Guide" —

In this anti-Christian culture that sexualizes women on every newsstand, Doug Giles comes to us as a pastor and maverick, teaching Christian dads how to train their daughters to be warriors for the Kingdom of God as well as the powerful self assured woman that knows who she is in Christ and how to defend herself spiritually and physically from any guy who thinks otherwise! Bravo my brother for showing us what the rest of a Prov. 31 woman looks like in this day and age!

— Brad Stine
"God's Comic" comedian/actor/author —

Doug Giles has scored another K.O. with "Raising Righteous and Rowdy Girls." Throughout this page-turner, his unique blend of wit, wisdom and irreverent humor is sharpened to a razor's edge. He slices and dices a godless culture, hell-bent on sexing-up and dumbing-down our sisters and daughters. As the father of two young girls, I can say this: Doug puts in print what every Christian dad thinks but may be afraid to say.

— Matt Barber,
Director of Culture Affairs, Liberty Counsel —

Doug Giles is my go to guy when I need cutting edge, no nonsense commentary and analysis on the events of the day. He is a modern day David slaying the gods of political correctness. His take is guaranteed to deliver a blow to the solar plexus that will leave his audience speechless. When it comes to parenting he knows what he's doing. His daughter Hannah is a chip off the old block, the kind of champion for Christ we should all be raising. Open your eyes and ears you might learn a thing or two from Doug!

— Pat Campbell
Host of The Pat Campbell Show, Tulsa, OK —

Our kids don't arrive with an instruction manual, but Doug Giles provides one for dads helping raise daughters. Fasten your safety belt, start reading, and prepare for paternal enlightenment! One other helpful feature: there's "No Assembly Required!"

— J.D. Hayworth
Broadcaster and Former Congressman —

Doug Giles

Raising Righteous and Rowdy Girls

Tiger Mom Meet Lion Dad!

Published by White Feather Press. (www.whitefeatherpress.com)

ISBN 978-0-9831751-2-4

Printed in the United States of America

Cover design by David Bugnon - mobopolis.com"

Cartoons by artist Doug Giles

White Feather Press

Reaffirming Faith in God, Family, and Country!

Dedication

This book is dedicated to all the former hell-raising fathers who now have a little daughter to look after. May God grant you great success in keeping them far away from guys like we used to be. Can I get a witness?

CONTENTS

Foreword

It has been said that daughters are God's revenge on fathers for the kind of men they were when they were young. Some would say that both Doug Giles and I, given our infamous pasts, are charter members of that club. However, Doug and I know that his two wonderful daughters and my equally wonderful daughter and two granddaughters are truly God's fantastic gift. With the wisdom of hindsight and experience, Doug has written the ultimate manual for dads on raising righteous and rowdy daughters who will go out into the world well prepared – morally, physically, intellectually and with joyful hearts – to be indomitable and mighty lionesses in our cultural jungle. Through every raucous and no-holds-barred page, Doug, the incomparable Dad Drill Sergeant, puts mere men through the paces to join the ranks of the few, the proud, and the successful fathers of super daughters. The proof of Doug Giles' gold-plated credentials are Hannah and Regis Giles – two of the most fantastic, great hearted and accomplished young ladies I have ever known. This is THE BOOK that I will be giving the father of my two precious five and three year old granddaughters. Tiger Mom meet Lion Dad!

— Pat Caddell
Fox News Contributor —

I originally penned this book, under a different title, back in 2007 to be published the following year by a "major" Christian publishing house. For some mysterious reason it got dropped. I got paid for it, which was cool, but it didn't hit the bookshelves, which sucked, until now, which is interesting.

From 2008 through the summer of 2009 my agent, poor guy, tried to sell this screed to several different publishers but alas, no takers. I heard from the various houses stuff like, "What makes this guy an expert on raising daughters? He's not Oprah, Dr. Phil, Mr. Rogers or Dr. Spock. He's not a pediatrician. He's a mouthy, gun-toting, bible thumping, cigar smoking red neck. I couldn't careless what he has to say about raising chickens much less girls." I heard it all and disappointment ruled my literary roost, at least as far as this project was concerned.

Then September 10th 2009 came along. On that blissful day, while I was speaking at a men's powwow in the wickedly gorgeous city of Vail, Colorado, my nineteen year old daughter, Hannah, was in New York City on *The Glenn Beck Show* dropping the first of several undercover investigative video bombs on ACORN's vapid head. For the uninitiated, ACORN was on Obama's short resume as his main claim to fame for why he should run this nation.

Yep, it was my daughter, Hannah Giles, who conceived the ACORN sting op and along with James O'Keefe, they posed as a pimp and a prostitute and videoed ACORN employees in multiple cities, all too giddy to aid and abet this sex trafficking duo in the establishment of whorehouses, in your backyard, staffed with thirteen year old sex slaves from El Salvador. How nice. Not!

When our nation saw these videos you could hear from the halls of congress to the hills of Hollywood a massive gasp and then a very loud, What the %$#@! The nation was stunned and outraged at ACORN's employees zeal and nonchalance in assisting these would be child abusers in milking the system while helping these faux criminals get a home loan, with our tax dollars, to whore out children.

Not only was the general public aghast at this evil bollocks but also since the release of the first video on September 10, 2009 the Census Bureau declared it was severing all ties with ACORN. The Senate voted 83-7 in favor of de-funding the controversial group. The House voted 345-75 to cut all funds to ACORN, and more than 20 states have demanded either a full investigation of ACORN or that they lose their funding. The IRS cut their connections to the group, and just recently ACORN has declared bankruptcy and announced it will undergo an official name-change.

As ACORN imploded and the morons in media attempted to slaughter Hannah for doing the job they were unable, if not unwilling to do, and as Hannah began receiving many national and international awards people began to wonder what made this teenager tick. And then my phone began to ring. And then major talk show hosts and various groups around the nation wanted to know how my wife and I raised such a courageous, poised under pressure, young lady.

About the time the media started the probe into the inner workings of Hannah's indomitable spirit her sister Regis' star began to rise in the hunting world being published in the NRA's *American Hunter* magazine, becoming a regular contributor to NRA's *InSight* magazine, a speaker at CPAC (the nation's largest conservative gathering), owner of her own company *GirlsJustWannaHaveGuns.com* and she's currently working on her forthcoming hunting and fishing television show slated for broadcast in 2012.

With two Giles girls cranking on all eight cylinders folks became really interested in what we put in our kids drinking water because Giles not only hit a home run with Hannah but Regis is now kicking butt and taking names as well. People began to ask "What did you do to keep your kids faithful to God and fearless in life, especially in this crappy culture and doubly especially in dealing with intense pressure from antagonistic forces?"

Well ladies and gents, herein lies the master list of what I made certain my baby's had cranking through their heart and soul as they began to bump up against life and all it's brutalities. It's not pretty but it worked. And it worked in a big way. And it worked in Miami that is famously known for vice. And it worked under virulent media attacks, death threats, and against multimillion-dollar lawsuits.

— Doug Giles —

Introduction
The Give a Flip Factor

Father, have you been to the mall lately and watched an unsupervised group of teenage girls get hit on by the ubiquitous male oxygen thieves? Pretty disturbing, eh? What's even more mind numbing is the number of beautiful young ladies who actually give these scat-based boys the time of day. Unreal. Ticks you off now, doesn't it?

If you have a pre-teen niña, then more than likely, after watching those mall chicks capitulate to the weird male critter's advances, you probably just swore to God that your daughter will never grow up to be one of "those girls" who would give one of those yard apes a second glance.

What about the junk on TV, dad? Have you switched on the idiot box and surfed around and seen the outrageous, can't-scrape-it-off-your-shoe compost the Manhattan marketing morons are trying to sell your young Sally before she hits puberty?

In the last few years Hollywood, public schools and universities, and fashion magazines have succeeded in making your girl feel weird if:

She doesn't sleep with a few chicks.

She doesn't make out with everything that moves.

She doesn't embrace being bad (as good is so, so passé, and being a slut, well that's totally awesome). It's empowerment!

She doesn't sleep with her zit-faced boyfriend, or at least dole out some fellatio, lest he become irate for being left high and dry. Yes, if she doesn't service the young squire, he might get angry and shoot up the school or church or something.

She doesn't drive drunk (heck, Paris, Britney, Lindsay and Chloe have done it and it appears they're okay, right? I mean...they're still on TV and look pretty and stuff, so...it can't be all that bad, now can it?)

She has problems with having a kid when she's a kid.

She doesn't take nude photos and videos of herself and send them around the planet via her cell phone, Facebook and Twitter.

She doesn't flash her breasts, make out with another girl and/or masturbate on camera all for the prized Girls Gone Wild T-Shirt.

She hasn't contemplated having kids out of wedlock when she's older because...y'know...Halley Berry did it, and marriage can be so, so complicated.

She doesn't turn into a horny Desperate Housewife who'll cheat on her husband with Julio the teenage pool boy.

She doesn't inflate her chest to a basketball's proportions.

She has thin lips and doesn't inject fat from her butt to plump 'em up.

She won't date a moron like Flava Flav in order to get on TV, or easy street, or at least capture the keys to a Honda Accord.

She has a problem with being a stripper.

She has a problem being like one of Hef's splooged brain girl-friends who'll have sex with a well-to-do octogenarian simply for his drachmas.

She has a problem with wearing a thong when she's 10 years old or donning a Halloween porn costume for her middle school party.

If I were a woman I'd be pretty ticked as it appears that "secular progressives" within America have succeeded in making young women known and appreciated only if they're a mud flap girl, a veritable catch rag for our orgasm-obsessed Onans. The empowered woman of today, dad, is the girl who wears a Hustler T-shirt, will strip on command, and has no problemo whatsoever in turning their vaginas into a sexual turnstile. Good job, you secular "progressive" weeds.

As you can imagine, buying into this sexed-up culture of raunch has caused an insane increase in STDs amongst our nation's teens. Yep, the reality is, my brother, that every twenty-four hours 21,000 teens are slapped, saddled, infused and infected with some creepy, nasty and potentially deadly bug brought about by following the advice of VH1.

It seems as if schlepping to the drum of the sexual revolutionaries of the '60s, American Pie, Superbad, Paris, and Pam has brought about a veritable venereal tsunami of which our teens are now drowning in the disease-laden wake.

The truth of the matter is that STDs are cranking in our culture like never before, and they are an equal opportunity infector. An estimated 19 million new cases occur each year with our kids getting hammered with the lion's share of this slop (teens now make up 25%

of the 19 million new "victims" annually).

Check out this smattering of factual 411 from Dr. Meg Meeker's new book *Your Kids at Risk: How Teen Sex Threatens Our Sons and Daughters*:

- This year, 8 to 10 million teens will contract an STD.

- Nearly one out of four sexually active teens is living with a sexually transmitted disease at this moment.

- Nearly 50% of African-American teenagers have genital herpes.

- Although teenagers make up just 10% of the population, they acquire 25% of all STDs.

- Herpes (specifically, herpes simplex virus type 2) has sky-rocketed 500% in the past 20 years among white teenagers.

- One in five children over the age of 12 tests positive for herpes type 2.

- Nearly one out of ten teenage girls has Chlamydia, and half of all new Chlamydia cases are diagnosed in girls 15 to 19 years old.

- STDs accounted for 87% of all cases reported of the top ten most frequently reported diseases in the United States in 1995.

This new epidemic is not just cursing those "poor inner city kids." No, the viruses have solidly taken up residence in the suburbs.

Moving from the STD stick our kids are being clobbered with, we have the threat of violence shooting through the roof, in particular, the violence leveled at our fair lasses.

According to the National Center for Missing and Exploited Children, of the 270 missing kids in Florida (as of 3/25/2008), 191 are girls. In addition, one out of every five teen girls will experience some form of dating violence by the time she finishes high school. Richie Cunningham's *Happy Days* are officially over, and our girls have got to wise up if they want to avoid being X chromosome carnage on our public pavement.

Heck, our kids aren't even safe in places where, in my day (I'm 48), safety was 99.9% given. What places am I referring to? I'm talking about schools and churches. Those two institutions, especially our schools, have pretty much gone down the crapper as far as being a safe haven for our kids because gun-wielding cretins have figured out that gun-free zones are opportunity-rich environments for them to carry out their dirty deeds.

Never in our nation's history have we seen students in schools mass murdered like we have in our recent history as a nation. For those who have short-term memory loss, here's a memory-stoking macabre list of what we've experienced in the last 20 years.

Stockton massacre – Stockton, California, January 17, 1989

University of Iowa shooting – Iowa City, Iowa, November 1, 1991

Simon's Rock College of Bard shooting – Great Barrington, Massachusetts, December 14, 1992

East Carter High School shooting – Grayson, Kentucky, January 18, 1993

Richland High School shooting – Lynnville, Tennessee, November 15, 1995

Frontier Junior High School shooting – Moses Lake, Washington, February 2, 1996

Pearl High School shooting –Pearl, Mississippi, October 1, 1997

Heath High School shooting – West Paducah, Kentucky, December 1, 1997

Jonesboro massacre – Jonesboro, Arkansas, March 24, 1998

Thurston High School shooting – Springfield, Oregon, May 21, 1998

Columbine High School massacre – near Littleton, Colorado, April 20, 1999

Heritage High School shooting – Conyers, Georgia, May 20, 1999

Santana High School shooting – Santee, California, March 5, 2001

Appalachian School of Law shooting – Grundy, Virginia, January 16, 2002

Rocori High School shooting – Cold Spring, Minnesota, September 24, 2003

Red Lake High School massacre – Red Lake, Minnesota, March 21, 2005

Campbell County High School shooting – Jacksboro, Tennessee, November 8, 2005

Platte Canyon High School shooting – Bailey, Colorado, September 27, 2006

Weston High School shooting – Cazenovia, Wisconsin, September 29, 2006

Amish School massacre – Nickel Mines, Lancaster County, Pennsylvania, October 2, 2006

 Henry Foss High School shooting – Tacoma, Washington, January 3, 2007

Virginia Tech massacre – Blacksburg, Virginia, April 16, 2007

Success Tech Academy shooting – Cleveland, Ohio, October 10, 2007

New Life Church shooting - Colorado Springs, Colorado, December 2007

Youth With a Mission Training Center shooting – Arvada, Colorado, December 2007

Louisiana Technical College shooting – Baton Rouge, Louisiana, February 8, 2008

Mitchell High School shooting – Memphis Tennessee, February 11, 2008

E.O. Green School shooting – Oxnard, California, February 12, 2008

Northern Illinois University shooting – DeKalb, Illinois, February 14, 2008

And I expect it to get worse as entitled and dysfunctional, whiny teenage toads are skating off un-rebuked for their bad behavior within our therapeutic, excuse-laden/BS enriched environment.

All of the above, the hot air on TV, the escalation of STDs and the boom in jackanapes with guns who'll strafe their mates for making fun of the pimple on their chin, makes you want to get a lifetime supply of beef jerky, MREs, several AK-47s and move your wife and kids to a bunker six hours north of nowhere, doesn't it?

I understand the desire to move to a remote location and isolate your family from this defunct civilization. And I've thought about doing it many times. However, I'm not one to retreat. I'm a finger flying, gravity defying Texas redneck rebel who would rather live in defiance than duck and run. One cannot live fleeing from bad things all their life or they'll end up living at Ted Kaczinsky's shack in Light a Fart, Wyoming.

I believe the key to raising girls that will not end up being a chunk of the flotsam in our societal swamp is for the parents (in particular the dad) to simply and sacrificially give a flip about their daughter's life. I call it the GAFF: The Give a Flip Factor. This is the Star Gate to raising stunning girls.

Listen, I don't care where you hail from, big daddy; if you're not nuttier than a squirrel turd and are engaged in making sure your baby is emotionally, physically, and spiritually healthy, then she'll be okay even if you guys live next door to Dennis Rodman. Conversely, you can move to Mayberry RFD and if you disengage from your girl, trust me, she'll find plenty of junk to get into in your "family friendly" city.

Yep, I believe engaged parents with traditional convictions can raise righteous and rowdy girls no matter how rank the environment is, but it won't be easy. This is war, old man, and it must be fought with parental passion and persistence, fueled by God's power and His proven wisdom 24/7 and 365. This must be done from the time your darling pops out of mamma's belly until you give her hand in marriage to some worthy dude.

Raising Righteous and Rowdy Girls is here to help you, my brother. Herein, I table scores of road-tested, historically proven, can't miss principles for raising girls with a fighting spirit, discernment, a winning attitude, and a holy vision to overcome this feces filled culture.

You will learn in the following finger-burning pages how to teach your daughters to fight, shoot guns, sense BS, be classy, despise anti-intellectualism, be visionaries, party without going Britney, to value hunting and the outdoors, the importance of traditional convictions, and how to avoid the date from hell.

Being the nice, honorable man that I am, I'll also toss in my 10 Commandments for My Daughter's Potential Boyfriend and an Application to Date My Daughter. I'm amazing.

These positive, powerfully primal "musts" will by fiat keep your butterfly away from the stupid son-of-a-monkey types who would seek to do her harm and derail her from her potentially awesome future.

This book doesn't come from the keyboard of some shrink or some weepy dude hooked on Oprah but rather from a Texas redneck who has been transplanted to Miami with two daughters who refused to let them become part of the local teen fart cloud.

My book is crude, rude, and now ... socially unacceptable. It is also biblically based, to the point, from the hip, short and sweet and attitude laden. A veritable choppy, roughly written compendium of counterculture credos for the traditionalist father who no likey what our society has become and who definitely doesn't want his lambs to become soiled by it. It might not be the smoothest book you've ever read, but it will work in raising counterculture kiddos.

So far, my wife and I have been pretty successful in our endeavors with our fillies, as our chicas are sharp, solid and smart young ladies who have a great balance between being a lady and being able to open up a can of some serious whup ass if need be. Unless you've been living under a rock or you're a liberal (but I repeat myself) you might have heard of one of my girls, Hannah Giles. She played the prostitute in the undercover ACORN sting videos which saved you billions and speeded along the investigation of this nefarious seedy organization. My other daughter has just broken on the national scene via *American*

Hunter magazine the spring of 2010. Yeah, that's right. She's a hunter, a conservationist and a gun freak. Be afraid Nancy boys.

Now, before you proceed on, father, do you have the GAFF when it comes to the welfare of thy little lady? If you do, this book is going to be gas to your flame. If not it will - if you're open to rebuke - increase your concerns for your child. However, if you're a dilatory dad who is obsessed with a mistress, concerned only with cash and who joneses on keeping up with the Joneses, this book is going to be harder to swallow than stewed rat is to Martha Stewart.

(Warning: The next chapter is kind of brutal if you have blown off your responsibility as a dad. Matter of fact, you might want to put on a cup.)

Raising Righteous

and Rowdy Girls

ONE

Strong Words for Weak Dads

I was channel surfing the other day when I landed on some hip hop music video. It was your basic Stooge-a-Palooza reel.

The scene was typical: The "musicians" and their homies (or "evolutionary holdovers," as I like to call them) were wearing T-shirts that would be too large for Hogzilla and sporting baseball caps pulled down over their ears like some Fat Albert character. In addition, they all had iced out/gold teeth grills, a prerequisite for the Cult of the Absurd.

These hoodlums also donned the Dennis Rodman multinecklace starter kit, cubic zirconium earrings, and, of course, tennis bracelets. Y'know, nothing screams, "I'm a bad ass!" more than stud earrings and costume jewelry.

Weighted down with all their bling, these creative geniuses launched into waving their beer bottles in the air like they just don't care as they sang/spoke their song so fast they'd make an espresso'd-up Joe Pesci sound like a groggy Slingblade.

The thing that floored me was not the musical gruel these dasypygals peddled, but all the gorgeous girls who were a part of these miscreants' music video.

Dozens of beautiful teens and twenty-something girls were wearing boy shorts and push-up bras as they writhed on the ground and on the hoods of cars as these "artists" poured beer on them, slapped them around, and simulated sex acts with them—with somebody's daughter! Which left me thinking, Where the hell are these girls' parents? In particular, where are their begetters?

Father, if your lass is working in one of these music videos, or posting nude pictures of herself on Facebook, or bearing it all for a Girls Gone Stupid DVD, or surgically inflating her chest to ocean-buoy proportions, then you have clearly not done your job as a father.

Hey, sperm donor, listen up: If you bring a little girl into this world, then it is your job to make certain she's got two feet firmly planted on terra firma. That's right, Pappy...you are the principal player in keeping your young woman from being the next Anna Nicole Smith.

I have two daughters. One is taking over the world, and the other is about to join her. When these female charges popped out of their mommy's womb years ago, this thing called "responsibility for their upbringing" hit me like a nun chuck.

> Hey! Sperm Donor! Listen up! Now you're a dad!

I didn't sluff off my role in their lives onto my wife, my church, public school, day care, relatives, TV, or "the village." I didn't expect any of them to fill my boots. I, along with my lovely wife, got my daughters here, and damn it, it's our job—especially my job as alpha male of the Giles castle—to prepare them internally and externally for greatness.

Living in Miami, I knew I would have to pony up and be a major player in my little one's lives if I wanted them to escape being part of the local teen wasteland. I knew I'd have to pay attention to them and spend time with them to instill them with solid values and principles. In other words, I was going to have to be a dad in the traditional sense of the word. Isn't that weird?

Call me goofy, but I don't want my nippers being inept, stressed out, unconfident young women who hate their bodies, get easily depressed, have no self-esteem, and will likely have issues with their weight. Also, I want to diminish the chances that my girls bail out of school or bow and kiss the ring of some abusive boyfriend or husband.

In addition, I'd like to make certain that my daughters never flaunt their bodies to get the attention of some Darwinian-throwback-gold-toothed-rapping-thug just so they can be the chief hoochie in his stupid booty video.

Furthermore, as my daughters' dad, I'd like to reduce the possibility that they'll ever become sex objects—or pregnant teens. I do not want my chicas becoming STD wagons or teens who do dope and abuse booze. I'd like to make certain that they've got a snowball's chance in Miami of ever seeing that junk occur in their lives.

What about you, Papasan? Would you like to guarantee your girl doesn't end up being YouTube's slut of the month? You would? Good for you. Then keep reading.

Pay Attention 007

Padre, I've got some advice for you. Mind if I share it? Great, here it is: Do not disengage from your daughter. Hang around your home and let your girl know (by your actions) that you really care about her, while showing her maximum affection.

That's right, you must cherish, coach, and guard your niña. Got it?

A lack of mental, physical, and spiritual input from you, Daddy-o, will exponentially boost the odds that your youngster will grow up to be more lost than Jenna Jameson sitting in an English Lit class discussing the symbolism in Kafka's *Metamorphosis*.

> YOUR LADY CANNOT RAISE YOUR DAUGHTER ALONE!

If you do not want your daughter to end up like Lindsay Lohan or Britney Spears and would, instead, like to raise a sharp, solid, and smart señorita, then you, dad, must get off your butt and get caught up in your girl's life.

Your lady cannot raise your daughter alone—and even if she could, she doesn't bring to the table what a man does. Period. I don't care what any feminist sociology teacher at Columbia says or what rancid Rosie propagates. Single moms, as good as some of them are, or lesbians (no matter how masculine they look and act) do not give your daughter what an involved father does.

Feminism would love for us all to believe that the dad's role in his daughter's life really isn't that important and that a dad can be easily replaced by lesbians, or public school, or Hillary's "village." This is the Kool-Aid being served to postmodern society, and, unfortunately, many people are drinking this poison and asking for seconds.

I beg to differ with these delirious dames and the dullards who parrot their opinions. No person is more important to a girl's well-modulated existence than a dad who's got his act together. A father who exhibits the God-given features of the alpha male is an irreplaceable ingredient in the recipe for a truly lovely and lively lady.

The 411 on Dads and Daughters

When a little girl has in her life a loving dad who is a provider, protector, hunter, and hero, research shows that sweet baby is going to turn into one amazing lady. When a great pappy's in the house, these are the kinds of reports you hear:

- Toddlers securely attached to fathers are better at solving problems.

- Six-month-olds scored higher on tests of mental development when their dads were involved in their lives.

- With dads in the home, kids managed school stress better.

- Girls whose dads provide warmth and control achieve higher academic success.

- Girls who are close to their fathers exhibit less anxiety and withdrawn behaviors.

The good news doesn't stop there. As the little darling matures and plows into puberty and beyond with a dad who's worth his salt at her side, these young women show these not-too-shabby traits:

- The likelihood that daughters engage in premarital sex, drug use, and alcohol plummets when their dads are involved in their lives.

- Girls with doting fathers are more assertive.

- Daughters who feel that their dads care about them and feel connected with their dads have significantly fewer suicide attempts and fewer instances of body dissatisfaction, depression, low self-esteem, substance abuse, and unhealthy weight.

- Girls involved with dad are twice as likely to stay in school.

- A girl's self-esteem is best predicted by her dad's loving affection.

You want me to go on? Because I can. You do? Here are some more factoids that you won't get from the liberal father-despising universities or their lockstep TV shows that dine on their propaganda swine:

- Girls with a dad or male father figure feel more protected, have higher self-esteem, are more likely to attempt college, and are less likely to drop out of college.

- Girls with fathers involved in their lives have higher quantitative and verbal skills and higher intellectual functioning.

- Girls whose parents divorce or separate before they turn twenty-one tend to have shorter life spans by four years.

- Girls with decent dads are less likely to flaunt themselves to seek male attention.

- Fathers help daughters to be more competent, more achievement oriented, and more successful.

- Girls with involved fathers wait longer to initiate sex and have lower rates of teen pregnancy. Teen girls who live with both parents are three times less likely to lose their virginity before their sixteenth birthday.

- 76 percent of teen girls said their fathers influenced their decisions on whether they should become sexually active.

- 97 percent of girls who said they could talk to their parents had lower teen pregnancy rates.

- A daughter from a middle-class family has a fivefold lower risk of out-of-wedlock pregnancy if her father lives at home.

- Girls who live with their mothers only have significantly less ability to control their impulses, delay gratification, and have a weaker sense of right and wrong.

- Kids do better academically when their fathers establish rules and exhibit affection.

The above bullet points were taken from Meg Meeker's book; *Your Teens at Risk*. Stop what you are doing now and log on to Amazon. com and buy one!

Hey Dad, here's a little FYI for you: Your little debutante has been birthed in the middle of a culture that would love to turn your little lady into a pirate hooker. Not only do we have insane terrorists longing to destroy us, but we also have the internal menace and constant rot of an anything-goes culture that you must equip your girl to stand against rather than succumb to.

I don't know about you, pa, but it would absolutely gut me to see my daughters dip into the crud this culture is laden with. Gone are the days of harmless partying, mild misbehaving, and good, clean fun. Thanks to the internet, TV, movies, video games, and an accommodation of a BS-bloated society, our little misses are now exposed to stuff that only the randiest sailors on leave in Borneo used to see and hear.

You can "call me a relic, call me what you will, say I'm old-fash-ioned, say I'm over the hill" but I'm determined

> *Screw this cul-ture and the liberals it rode in on!*

not to go with the flow of this foul and feckless culture. I'm not going to be hip and groovy. I decided many years ago not to capitulate like other ignorant and spineless parents have to this culture and instead to raise my girls to be proper ladies in the traditional sense of the word. Screw this culture and the liberals it rode in on.

Yes, I admit it: I am a freak. I'm the weird one because I don't want my girls to be a part of the one in five Americans past the ripe old age of twelve who tests positive for herpes. Nor do I want them to be a part of the 12 percent who will be victims of rape, nor part of the 40.9 percent of girls who are forced by their bogus boyfriend to have sex lest they make him mad, nor be a part of the incredibly multiplying STD crew. But that's just me.

Yes, brother, I want my girls and yours to be secure enough not to follow the hellish herd that has a monopoly on stupidity. I want my daughters to have fun in life, living a clean, no-regret existence as they forego folly in all its forms. I want my daughters to forget that stuff about learning from their mistakes. I want them to realize that it is cheaper and far more entertaining to learn from Amy Winehouse's mistakes.

Raising Girls Who Rock

As you can tell, Mr. Rogers I am not. I am Mr. Rager. Why do I rage against the machine? Well, I'm ticked off because of all the pa-rental passivity I see—moms and dads passing their duties to TV or a Portuguese nanny because they're "too busy" working on their tan, obsessing over work, or they're preoccupied with Facebook.

A few years ago, comedian Dennis Miller proposed a bill for would-be parents. The bill would be similar to the Brady Bill, which requires a five-day waiting period/background check before a person can purchase a firearm. This bill would be called the Brady Bunch Bill and would require a couple who wanted to have a child to swear to God and on their mother's grave that once they bring a child into the world, they'd do their best to make certain their child does not become a miscreant zombie. 2

> Mr. Rogers I am not. I am Mr. Rager!

Dad, you'll see as I roll out this bad boy that raising girls who rock isn't rocket science. So relax. You won't have to start watching Oprah, Rachel Ray, the Lifetime Channel, or read every flippin' issue of *Parenting* magazine in order to assist your girl. The basic thing you need—the one thing you must have—is simply to care about her. If you're actually and actively concerned about your children in today's culture of parental narcissism, you will have set yourself apart from the pack and are on course for keeping your daughter from being the next train wreck featured on the local evening news.

TWO

Teach Your Daughter How to Fight

June 2, 2007—Police in Overland Park, Kansas are seeking information about a vehicle and person of interest in the disappearance of an eighteen-year-old girl. Kelsey Smith was last seen being pushed into her car in a parking lot after leaving a discount store.

Kelsey dropped by the Target store by the Oak Park Mall to buy supplies for her graduation party. She was seen entering and leaving the store wearing a pink tank top and black shorts, but she never made it home, where she was expected to meet her boyfriend at 7:20 PM Saturday.

Piecing together images from several cameras in the area, police have developed the following timeline:

Kelsey Smith's gray 1987 Buick enters the Target parking lot. Shortly afterward, a black older model Chevrolet pickup enters the lot.

Kelsey is captured on surveillance entering the store. She is later shown on another camera at the checkout purchasing wrapping paper and other items.

A white man, about six feet, 175 pounds, and in his twenties, wearing a white T-shirt, black shorts, and black converse tennis shoes walks out of the Target store. He has short dark hair and a goatee.

Kelsey leaves the store with the items she purchased and walks to her car, just a few parking spaces from the entrance of the store.

Someone dressed like the man mentioned above approaches Kelsey near the rear of her car. What happens is unclear because the tape is grainy, but it appears a scuffle takes place and Kelsey is forced into her own vehicle.

Kelsey's vehicle is found by her grandparents two hours later across the street in the parking lot of a mall. Her purse and packages were still inside.

Shortly after her vehicle is discovered, the black pickup truck is seen on another camera leaving the area.

Kelsey's car is being processed for possible evidence, but so far no information is available.

* * *

June 7, 2007—Searchers find the body of Kelsey Smith in a shallow creek about twenty miles from where she disappeared. Investigators are not yet releasing any details concerning evidence in the case.

"This community has lost a vibrant and promising life and a family has suffered unimaginable tragedy," Johnson County prosecutor Phil Kline said.

What if Kelsey could have defended herself? I guarantee she didn't go shopping on June 2nd thinking, This'll be the day that I die. Knowing self-defense probably would have saved her life.

What Would Your Daughter Do?

What about your daughter? Could she handle herself if she were attacked by some thug?

Etiquette flew out the window twenty years ago, and our neighborhoods are now seeing perverts and pedophiles aplenty. Young and old men alike behave like groping, brutish, and offensive horn dogs who would love nothing more than to get gross with our daughters.

I am not cool with this.

And should some perp cross the line by threatening my daughters' lives, I would have no problem personally pounding him into the

> *My babies know how to render a bad guy severely inoperative!*

10

pavement for the glory of God and the betterment of mankind. In my family, I am alpha dog: provider, protector, hunter, and hero.

Even though I wouldn't bat an eye or lose a nanosecond of sleep sending some sack of slop to an early grave, I do, sadly, realize that I am not omnipresent and that my daughters are going to have to rely upon themselves as the first line of defense.

Since I would never want one of my darlings to be at the mercy of one of these hell-bent toads, I have made certain that my babies know how to render a bad guy severely inoperative and, if need be, kill him.

Not even out of their teens, both of my daughters are assistant instructors in Jiu-Jitsu and have extensive training with knives and guns; they have the ability to use and remove these weapons from a mentally defective dude who might have to die in order to learn something. This is my definition of girl power: girls having the attitude, skill, and force to pulverize a felonious punk.

Why am I insistent about having daughters who are able to fight? Well, it's principally because of these eight statistics:

1. One rape or sexual assault occurs every two minutes.

2. One violent crime occurs every five seconds in the US.

3. 172 women are physically and/or sexually assaulted every hour.

4. 261,000 rapes and sexual assaults occurred in the US in 2000.

5. 90,186 forcible rapes were reported to police in 2000.

6. In a six-month US Department of Justice study, 2.8 percent of college women experienced rape.

7. 83 percent of rape or sexual assault victims were victimized by someone they knew.

8. One murder occurs every 34 minutes.

Here's what I'm doing to make sure, as much as I can, that this stuff doesn't happen to my girls. First off, being a Christian, I pray for my daughters' safety and trust God to keep the creeps at a distance. I'm not talking about "Now I lay me down to sleep . . ." prayers, but fire-breathing, paint-melting prayers where I boldly speak the protective covenantal promises God gave me in Scripture—loud enough to scare the hell out of any demonic forces that might want to jack with my girls.

> *Keep a good buffer zone between your-selves and the urchin!*

Second, I've told my babies (since life is so chock-full of male jerks) not to put themselves into the path of a bunch of ham-fisted Harrys when they know it's just a matter of milliseconds before one of the inbreeds says or does something that's going to escalate into something egregious.

Look, I'm not one to shy away from fights; in fact, I've made a great living being a provocateur. However, given that we live in a day of deep mental male density, my advice to my lovely ladies is to put as much distance between them and the guttersnipes as possible.

Dads, teach your girls that if they have to be around such saps, they should keep a good buffer zone between themselves and the urchin. It's simple: Where the thugs are, your daughters are not. If for some reason your girls must breathe the same air as these Darwinian leftovers, tell them to do it from across the room—I'm talkin' way across the room.

What your girl's gotta do is learn how to immediately size up people and situations. This doesn't mean they have to be paranoid freaks. It just means they're simply on the alert for mentally challenged chumps.

Should your daughter find that she is required to be in an unsafe place, then she should be fully conscious of the morons, keep her distance, do her business, and then split. In addition, encourage your daughter to have girl friends and guy friends with her who have a zero tolerance policy for zeroes and who will always have her back.

Third, I've made sure my daughters have the attitude to successfully send a "stay the hell away" message in whatever form necessary to stifle male mooks. Because now you can't go to Target to buy toothpaste without some jerkmeister stalking you and looking for an opportunity to duct tape you and throw you into the trunk of his '83 Camero for a *Silence of the Lambs* fantasy, you have got to be ready, darling. Thus, I pump my daughters full of attitude. Nowadays everything smells, so attitude sells.

> *A nonnegotiable for winning in life is attitude!*

A nonnegotiable for winning in life is attitude. It's also a nonnegotiable in crushing an attacker. You've got to have that "Don't tread on me" spirit. You dig? Attitude goes a long way toward helping you when things go way wrong.

For your ladies to survive and thrive around the sickos, they've got to have the mind-set that they will not be victimized. Their attitude lets the pervert know that they will have no trouble hurting him or sending him to an early roast on the second concentric circle of Dante's Hibachi. Of course, this doesn't mean she's gotta be rude all the time. Don't encourage your baby to put a nice guy in an Ellie Mae headlock just for asking her what time it is.

I suggest that when in a conflict situation, your girl hit the douche bag with words first. Start off with something like, "Touch me again and you'll wish you were at home cross dressing and sashaying to a Boy George CD." It's important that your girl doesn't laugh or blink or look away when she drops her verbal invectives upon the vile weed. She has got to be cold—I'm talkin' about making snotcicles hang off the dude's nose because she has chilled him so thoroughly.

If that doesn't work, and the guy persists...then I recommend that my dainties wale on him.

Before I go on, I want to speak directly to Christian dads for a sec: Can you forget the "turn the other cheek" stuff when it comes to your girl's personal defense? Look, I'm all for turning the other cheek when it comes to being verbally persecuted for your beliefs; however, when it comes to someone harming your darling, you should abandon the docile response and train your dainty girl to wield her mouth and hands with satanic precision.

Do not under any religious pretenses make your daughter a doormat for the demented. Remember, Christ whipped some butt in his day, and your girl should know when to be delicate and when to be deadly...when to be a lady and when to be lethal. It's your job, dad, to enable her to discern exactly when it's that time.

Now, because I do not believe in anyone being at the mercy of the merciless, as stated, my girls have been training in martial arts (namely Jui-Jitsu) from an early age—and not just any Jui Jitsu school, but the world-famous Gracie Jui-Jitsu school.

> *Christ whipped some butt in his day. Don't make your daughter a doormat for the demented!*

Yep, it's important that you don't toss your bird to just anybody to train her. Every Tom, Dick, and Harry has a Tae Kwon Do studio and will dole out a black belt for the right price. Not so with the Valente/Gracie boys. When you're talking about life-and-death situations, you must employ those who are masters at keeping your good girl alive and the bad boy dead...or at least wishing he was dead.

Fighting Jiu-Jitsu Style

Pedro Valente is the chief instructor at Valente Brothers Jiu-Jitsu in Miami, Florida. Seeing that he is an expert in kicking butt and training others to mangle the mendicant, I asked him to add his two cents to this chapter. Below is our exchange regarding training girls to fight Valente/Gracie Jiu-Jitsu style.

How does Jiu-Jitsu help women?

The techniques of Jiu-Jitsu are not based on strength and athleticism, but rather on an understanding of the human anatomy and the laws of physics and their application with the objective of offsetting the power of an attacker.

Jiu-Jitsu is referred to as the triumph of human intelligence over brute strength. Since women in general are physically weaker than men, they can make special use of these techniques in order to level

> *Jiu-Jitsu is the triumph of human intelligence over brute strength!*

the playing field in a critical situation. When properly trained in the art of defending against any imaginable physical attack, a woman feels confident that she can survive an act of aggression by a stronger and more powerful man.

At what age should a girl start her

training?

The younger, the better. Jiu-Jitsu is a great tool to increase the confidence and self-esteem of any child. At a young age, girls are frequently picked on by bullies, and these situations often create psychological trauma that can last a lifetime. Girls who are trained in Valente/Gracie Jiu-Jitsu have the poise to confront bullies and not be intimidated by them. The sooner they start, the easier it is for them to develop the reflexes and the automatic reactions that will enable them to apply the techniques naturally when they grow older.

> Using Jiu-Jitsu, girls can neutralize a man of superior size and strength.

Jiu-Jitsu is a natural art, and since kids are not physically strong, the learning process is faster and simpler when they are younger. My sister started learning Jiu-Jitsu when she was two years old.

How long before you can train a normal and healthy girl to defend herself?

The longer a girl trains, the more prepared she is going to be to face an attacker. Since women usually give up a significant physical handicap to men, they need to master each technique in order to use it effectively. However, after completing a fifty-lesson course, any woman will have the elements to defend herself against any man in any situation. After that it's a matter of continual practice with the objective of maximizing her odds of surviving an assault.

Can a small girl really defend herself against a big guy?

Yes, because the moves taught in Jiu-Jitsu are not dependent upon physical strength. Therefore, a girl will learn, through the techniques of Jiu-Jitsu, how to neutralize a bigger opponent's physical strength and actually use it to her advantage in many cases.

> Give your daughter permission to be rude.

What are the three most important things you teach a girl who wants to stop a goon?

First, speak with confidence and be assertive. Be outspoken giving yourself permission to be rude. Don't be nice to strangers. If you decide to attack your aggressor, do so quickly and with complete conviction. Attackers are most often cowards and prefer to attack easier and more submissive targets.

Second, don't panic! Stay as relaxed as possible and wait for the perfect opportunity to counterattack with the Jiu-Jitsu technique that best fits the situation you are in.

Third, always be alert and prepared. Remember that an assault does not have a set date and time like a professional fight, for example.

Can you relate a couple of examples of girls the Gracies trained who were actually attacked and how what you taught them caused them to disable their assailant?

Several female Jiu-Jitsu practitioners have related situations where they were able to avoid an assault through their assertive behavior and without the necessity of any physical confrontation. The confidence attained by girls who practice Jiu-Jitsu is so great that, in many cases, just the firmness in their eye contact causes their attacker to pick an easier target. Most attackers back out when they feel that the woman is willing to fight back and defend herself.

But there have been examples both in Brazil and the US where women have escaped physical assaults using the proven techniques of Valente/Gracie Jiu-Jitsu. One time, in Brazil, a rapist who was armed with a knife took a Jiu-Jitsu practitioner to the ground in a secluded area, and as he prepared to perform an act of sexual violence the woman applied an arm lock and managed to run away.

> *If someone looks suspicious, leave and go to a safe place.*

What are the top ten things you would tell a girl to do who has no training in Jiu-Jitsu or any other martial art?

- Trust your instincts. If someone looks suspicious to you, leave and get to a safe place. It's better to be cautious than wrong.

- Be familiar with your limitations and how you react under stress. Some women respond effectively by physical struggle or fighting; others by running; others by distraction, screaming, or talking. Know your personal style and get self-defense training to change or enhance that style if necessary.

- Realize that anyone who gets upset that you are suspicious of them may not have your best interest in mind.

- Be aware that assaults, including rape, can happen to any-one, anywhere, anytime. Always be aware of people and the environment around you.

- Don't drink alcohol or use illegal drugs. Feel free to say no to anything that makes you uncomfortable.

- Don't use a weapon unless you've been trained to use it.

- When walking, running, or jogging, don't use headsets— you can't hear someone approaching or signaling you.

- Always lock your car, even if you'll only be out a few min-utes.

- Always lock the car when in it, so no one can open the doors.

- If you think you're being followed by another car, don't pull into your driveway. Drive straight to the nearest po-lice or fire station and honk your horn. Don't leave your car until you're sure it's safe.

For more information about Valente Jui-Jitsu, you can reach them online at *www.valentebrothers.com*. Pedro, Gui, and Jimmy rock. If you live in Miami, do yourself a favor and join, ladies. I have seen firsthand what an awesome job they've done with my daughters!

How to Defend Yourself—Before It's Too Late

In addition to what Pedro has recommended, I've got to weigh in with some tips for girls who are getting accosted (being the loud-mouthed, opinionated guy I am) but do not know martial arts. Dads, read this list carefully and make sure your daughters know each of these ways to defend themselves when attacked.

- If some tool attacks you from the front, try to shatter his knee with your foot. I'm talkin' wash that sucker out! Don't be tentative; haul off and shatter that kneecap. Make it squishy.

- If an oxygen thief grabs you before you can kick the crap out of his knee, then jam your knee up into his crotch. Do this as hard as you can. Make him speechless by crushing his boys.

- If you've got free arms, don't just flail them around in the air. Use them, girlfriend, to punch his head. Wail on him. Punch his eyes, ears, nose, and throat. Smack his temple. Go ballistic! The throat is an awesome target. If you land a solid in the dude's throat, he will not be able to breathe. He'll feel like he's about to go meet Jesus.

- If you don't have enough space to throw a punch, then stab your fingers into his eyes; grab his lip and yank it down like you mean it; get hold of a finger and bend it back until you hear a snap; dig your fingers deep into his neck and try to pick his Adam's apple.

- If you can't move your arms or hands, you can bite him. You can also scream like a wild banshee.

- If he grabs you from behind, try to rip his balls from his body—grab, crush, and tear. Say that with me, "Grab, crush, and tear." One more time: "Grab, crush, and tear!" In addition, you can kick back hard into his knee with your heel, slide down the shin, and crush the instep of his foot.

- Joints bent in the wrong direction can be very painful. Grab every appendage you can and bend 'em backward— hard!

- Lastly, if your life is being threatened and you have a pistol and a concealed weapon permit, and are carrying said weapon when accosted...just shoot the bastard.

I'll Tase You, Bro!

If your doll doesn't know martial arts (yet), and she's not too confident about opening a can of whup ass on an assailant (yet), and she's not cool with guns (yet) you ought to think about getting her a taser.

As of late the taser is coming on strong. They're concealable, powerful and effective to the extent that their application to an offender usually ends the ordeal. Yes, most wussies can be beaten back by the simple administration of the taser terminals to their squishy man tits. In addition to being effective, it's fun to watch the guy vibrate on the ground like Curly when he didn't have any cheese.

Dana Leigh Shafman of *www.shieldher.com*, has made it her life's mission to make certain that women everywhere morph from being helpless little damsels in distress to being high-voltage honeys who'll zap your backside with a Taser C2 if you screw with them. To help accomplish this noble task, Dana has created not only her online company but also Taser Parties, through which her staff trains future Charlie's Angels on how to bug zap losers. You gotta love it. No Tupperware or toenails. Tasers and only tasers. Finally, a ladies' meeting that I would like to attend!

C'mon señor, make this the year in which your chica ceases to be a helpless victim. Whether she's in her car, classroom, store, her own house or in church, she must get packed, stacked and ready to whack because the fools today are bold and multitudinous. Yes, the apple of your eye must help society send a message to these evolutionary holdovers that she will rock them with a club, a kick, a gun (my favorite) or a taser for attempting to do her harm.

It's time that your girl stop relying on anyone else to defend her but herself. Therefore, encourage your darling to start martial arts, go to a gun class, or if she doesn't like blood and stuff, go to *www.shieldher. com*, buy her a taser, and have Dana and her girls host a Taser Party in your town to help Ms. Shafman spread the word to criminal turds that their day is done.

Note: Tasers are not legal to carry in all states. Check with the appropriate legal personnel before buying one.

Dead jack ass found double-tapped and dead on the curb!

I Have a Dream

I'm a dreamer. I can't help it. I've seen *The Lion King* too many times not to be a visionary. I have many dreams, desires and visions. One in particular is to hunt all of the big-five dangerous game animals in Africa. If I live long enough, by golly, I plan on making that happen. Here's another thing I'd like to see. Here's a dream I've been having lately.

I'd like to see a nationwide tsunami of ladies equipped to the teeth with the physical prowess and the firearm capability to kill any and all would-be murderers and rapists should such creeps ever accost them.

I have a dream!

A dream where girls walk in utter confidence amongst the masturbatory me-monkeys that surround them. A dream where women have solid assurance that they can and will serve some ham-fisted tool his own scrotum if need be.

I have a dream!

A dream where instead of reading about a cute college coed left dead and naked out in a vacant lot or bloated and floating in a river, the story reads, "dead jack ass found double-tapped and dead on the curb as his soul wings its way to hell, all because he messed with the wrong mama."

A dream where it's normal for girls to know Jiu-Jitsu and mixed martial arts. A dream where they can shoot golf ball sized groups with their .38 at 15 feet. A dream where they have a BS detector that's so sensitive they can read people and environments with godlike clarity within a nanosecond.

> *God speaks to me in a high-pitched, angry Chinese accent.*

I have a dream!

A dream where the Johan van der Sloots and all the other Bobbie Cutts-like splooge-brained droogies in the midst of us live forever in fear. A dream where parents will raise their daughters to be sweet and deadly dames.

I have a dream where if some douche bag in the name of his stupid religion ever abuses his wife or daughter and God doesn't strike him dead on the spot, that his wife or daughter will. Okay, maybe that's too extreme. How about put him in an irreversible coma?

I have a dream!

A dream where the tide turns in the news cycle and we start hearing reports of molesting men going to an early grave instead of a good girl. A dream where if a girl tells her buddies that a guy is bothering her, her friends scare the living daylights out of him. Can I get a witness?

I have a dream where Christian parents will flush this "turn the other cheek" stuff down the crapper once and for all when it comes to their daughter being assaulted by an autoerotic dung beetle trying to work out his groove.

I have a dream!

How did this dream come about? This holy vision came from God in direct response to my prayers over the cultural nightmare women in the US live with now.

How do I know it was God who spawned this afflatus? It was easy for me to know it was Him because every time He speaks to me (and it's quite often), it's always in a high-pitched, angry Chinese accent.

In addition to God birthing this vision within me, another factor gave rise to this would-be dream world of mine: I just realized that protective fathers, brothers, friends and bad-ass uncles aren't omnipresent (I know...I'm slow. I went to public school.), and therefore all girls everywhere have to rely upon themselves as their first line of defense.

Yes, since their gallant male counterparts can't be everywhere at all times to render aid, we've got to make certain that our babies know how to leave a bad guy severely inoperative and, if need be, kill him all by their lonesome. That is my definition of "girl power." This is my dream: all girls of every conceivable stripe having the attitude, skill, and force to pulverize a felonious punk.

I'd like to see the following:

- One million girls flooding into martial art classes
- One million girls getting handgun training
- One million girls purchasing their own piece and getting licensed to carry it
- One million girls getting a taser for the less egregious attacks
- One million girls getting a heavy dose of common sense to avoid, as much as possible, dangerous scenarios

This concludes my heavenly vision.

I know this chapter is not a pleasant topic to contemplate. Dads, it might be hard for you to think of your sweet, innocent baby girl beating the snot out of some guy. However, this is the world we live in, and to be forewarned is to be forearmed.

Think about how many girls would be alive and pursuing their desires today... if only they had known how to fight. And think of all the pimps and thugs who would be in jail or worse...if only their victims had known how to immobilize the imbeciles.

Given the violent culture we inhabit here in the United States of Acrimony, I have purposefully raised my daughters with this maxim: When the crap hits the fan, be the fan.

Dad, one of the greatest things you can give your girl is the ability to fight—to rock in a hard place—should the occasion ever arise. Be prepared.

THREE

Teach Your Daughter How to Shoot Guns

"Fear no man of any size, call on me and I'll equalize."

— Common engraving
on Frontier firearms —

Never bring a knife to a gun fight.

I was on a talk show the other day defending the Second Amendment and discussing with my host the stupid and un-constitutional D.C. gun ban. I made it clear that I am a Christian who is extremely cool (to the point of being giddy) with our right to keep and bear arms.

After we trounced the anti-gun lobby for their goofy, doe-eyed, John Lennon-like *Imagine* solutions to violent crime, we opened up the phone lines for folks to weigh in with their two cents. The first caller was a woman who asked if I thought Jesus would carry a weapon if He were here today, to which I quickly replied, yes, of course He would—especially if He lived in Miami and was driving down I-95 at four o'clock in the morning.

The female caller, being far more spiritual than I am, didn't think it was funny and went on to make it personal by asking if someone were attacking one of my daughters and I had a gun if I thought Christ would be cool with me killing the felonious freak. I told her that I sure hoped He would because otherwise He'd be terribly disappointed

> *Jesus is okay with me killing a felonious freak!*

in me and would just have to forgive me. Common sense and primal instinct tell me that the bad guy should die and the good girl should live. Call me carnal.

Of course the holier-than-me caller was aghast that as a Christian I would have no problem whatsoever defending my friends, family, person and possessions with deadly force. Her reason being was that she couldn't picture Jesus doing it and concluded that because she couldn't wrap her mind around Him green-lighting the destruction of a demented perp that He certainly wouldn't and thus I shouldn't.

When discussing what Christ would do in a given situation, it's usually good to actually go to the gospels, read them and then draw conclusions. Here's what I've gotten after scouring Scripture a few times:

1. Jesus in His earthly ministry didn't carry a weapon except the time when He took a whip (a whip! You gotta love it!) and Billy Jack'ed the televangelists out of the temple. He didn't chide them or write them a strong but tasteful e-mail asking them to please not do that kind of stuff in church.

   What did the meek and mild Messiah do? He whipped them. God, I hope you got that on DVD for me to watch when I get to heaven. I wonder if the Christ-is-a-pacifist-wuss-lady can picture sweet Jesus laying the leather to the backs of the marketers who were making His father's house a place of merchandise.

   If Christ were to do that today He'd be thrown in prison, and 99.9% of churches in the USA wouldn't have Him speak at their annual Hallelujah Aren't We Fabulous conference because Jesus wouldn't be behaving very "Christ-like."

2. It's clear from Scripture that Jesus didn't need weapons
    because He had at his disposal an angelic host that could
    flatten armies. I unfortunately don't have that capability.
    Nor can I walk through walls or split oceans. Christ had
    supernatural protection, and His disciples carried swords.
    I, too, believe that God supernaturally protects me, to
    some degree, because I should have been dead a long time
    ago. However, should my guardian angel be napping or
    busy doing something else other than trying to keep up
    with me, I'll be okay, because Smith & Wesson art with
    me as well.

3. Lastly, in Luke 22:36-38 Christ told his disciples, even
    though He personally did not pack a weapon, that they,
    in light of His departure, should get a deadly weapon—
    namely a sword. Check it out...

    > "And he [Jesus] said to them [His disciples], 'But now,
    > whoever has a money belt is to take it along, likewise also
    > a bag, and whoever has no sword is to sell his coat and
    > buy one. For I tell you that this which is written must be
    > fulfilled in Me, 'And he was numbered
    > with transgressors'; for that which refers
    > to Me has its fulfillment.' They said,
    > 'Lord, look, here are two swords.' And He
    > said to them, 'It is enough.'"

    Jesus told his
    disciples to car-
    ry a viscious,
    nasty and
    deadly weapon.

    Jesus told them—didn't ask or mildly sug-
    gest—but told His buddies to sell their leather
    jacket if need be and buy a sword. The sword
which Christ told his compadres to purchase was not a QVC decora-
tive Claymore to hang on their walls to commemorate the good times
they had when Christ was around. The original word used for sword
in this text was a large knife used for killing animals and cutting flesh.
It was particularly fashioned for short, deadly thrusts in hand-to-hand
combat.

Jesus didn't tell them to carry a whistle, a shofar horn, or a bag of
sand to blow in bad guys' eyes, but a dagger-like sword. A vicious, nas-

ty and deadly weapon not used for cutting vegetables, spreading butter or splitting a bagel but for violently tapping a lung or heart in case of an attack. Now, in a 21st century WWJD context, even though He didn't personally carry a weapon, what do you think He thinks about His followers defending themselves with deadly force, huh, pacifists?

The above was taken from my weekly column which I wrote for Townhall.com on March 1, 2008. Why did I include it here? Two reasons: 1. I was running short on my contractual word count. 2. I'd like to forever bury the notion that Jesus was a long-haired Gandhi in regard to self defense. Since my book comes from me, a Christian, and is written to people who, for the most part, sport a Christian worldview, and it is was originally to be published by one of the top dog Christian publishing houses, I thought it apropos to show Jesus has no problemo with guns and ammo.

Christian dad, if Christ is cool with His disciples carrying deadly force then I think we should be. It's a raw thought, but sometimes the times demand that a violent weed gets weeded off the earth if he won't leave good people the heck alone. Especially if said toad has our daughters in their crosshairs. I say the perp dies and our good girl lives. I don't play when it comes to my kid's life. She has the right to pursue happiness, and the criminal miscreant who accosts her has earned his right to go to hell sooner than he expected. What say you, pops?

Lock and Load

The carrying of a deadly weapon and the ability to have within your hand the wherewithal to remove a person from the planet is a sobering cup of Joe. I know you're thinking, "Why, thank you Captain Obvious. I wouldn't have seen that if you hadn't pointed it out to me."

Because the topic of sending a felonious wanker to an early grave is indeed grave, you need to sit down with your daughter and ask her this question: Would you shoot to kill a person if they were going to do you or others physical harm? Because, duh, that's the whole point of carrying a gun. She should have the attitude that, "I dont want to use it but should I have to I'm mentally prep'ed." If she's not psychologically "there" then you sure don't want

> *Carrying a deadly weapon is a sobering cup of Joe.*

to put a gun in her hands because it not only is useless (as she will not use it for what it is intended for, namely to kill a bad guy), but it also could be snatched out of her hand and used against her.

So, first things first, father: If your girl is going to carry a weapon or have one in her house, then she had better perform the proper mental gymnastics necessary for her to move into Dirty Harry mode if things should go to hell in her presence. There's no time for contemplation in such a situation. When the smack hits the fan, it happens fast. Is she ready?

> If she can't pull the trigger, she shouldn't own a gun.

If your daughter cannot see herself actually using the weapon she is carrying then she has no business having a piece on her person. Yep, she had better stick with knowing martial arts or sporting a Taser C2 or having Cujo go on the defense for her against the obstreperous because the prerequisite mindset for the serious gun owner is: I have no problem using it if a stupid, stupid felon forces my hand.

For those girls who have made the leap into the "I'll turn him into worm food and not bat a false eyelash" mode, let's talk about guns. This is one of my favorite topics: discussing with good folks the proper personal weaponry to sport so that they radically decrease the likelihood that they will ever be victimized by a dumb dude trying to hurt them.

Getting Started

Dad, before you get your girl a gun, take her to a gun store or a gun range where they have several calibers, makes and models to choose from and have her try all the ones that are made for self defense.

Start her on the small end of the caliber spectrum okay, Rad Magnum? It won't help things if she's christened with a .500 S&W, .454 Casull or a .50cal Desert Eagle. She'll develop a flinch worse than the one I have when I see Pelosi without makeup. Personally, I'd start her with a little .22 and have her build up to the .38 and 40 calibers.

> Let your daughter choose her own gun.

Let her run through the semi-autos and revolvers to see which one she digs the most. Most first-time femme fatales will go for the revolvers because they're pretty much a fluff and fold weapon as the automatics, for most novices, are just a little more complicated. Having said that, see which one she takes to. Remember, this is her gun, not yours, and the most important thing is her having a pistol that she is extremely comfortable with.

As most of you guys know, figuring out what a woman wants is more difficult than trying to get Donald Trump to watch Rosie O'Donnell River Dance naked. Having a-one-size-fits all approach to arming your ladies is not wise. Let them report. Let them decide.

> *She must practice until her gun skills are second nature.*

For example, every one of my ladies likes a different pistol. My wife is sweet on my AirLite Smith & Wesson .357 magnum revolver, but only with the .38 Special rounds. My oldest daughter takes a shining to my Sig Sauer .380 automatic, and my youngest daughter freaks over the Springfield .40cal auto. Go figure! It's your job, dad, to get them what they can handle and shoot with the greatest of ease. Trust me, for self-defense purposes, you want their comfort and confidence levels through the roof.

Once the caliber, model and action are decided upon, now it is time to shoot and shoot and shoot and shoot. For attack scenarios it's not necessary with a handgun for them to practice shooting targets at 1,000 meters. My law enforcement buddies say that in serious altercations the victim needs to be able to deftly deliver three shots in three seconds at three feet: 3-3-3 (I told you when "it" happens, it happens fast).

Therefore, go to work at close range and with rapid fire. If, God forbid, your baby gets into deep weeds, you want her to do the job properly; e.g., triple tap the center mass of the murderous/raping jackass. At least double tap it. Two or three shots in the center of the chest should officially end the happy day of your kid's enemy. Work with her 'til she's proficient in firing with both speed and accuracy. Help her to keep her shots tight, fast and not all over the map. Get several human silhouette targets and have her shoot for the center of the chest and keep her shots within the heart/lung area. To be effective in defense scenarios her gun skills must become second nature,

> The best bang for your buck is a 12-gauge shotgun!

and this comes only through practice, practice and practice.

Once she has attained confidence and crazy capability, go with her back to the gun range/ store and have her get a concealed weapons permit. With this she will be able to defend herself with deadly force almost everywhere she goes outside of her house. Speaking of her house ...

Y'know, small pistols are great for your person. However, for home defense you can step things up a notch. You don't have the concealed weapon problem when protecting yourself and your castle. Here's where the ultimate crime stopper comes into play: the shotgun. Same thing applies here, pops, as to her choice of scatterguns. Get her the one that she likey.

The best bang for the person's buck is the 12-gauge pump shotgun with an extended magazine. Most of your major manufacturers have one of these beauties available for the consumer. The barrel is short, 18.5 – 20 inches, the magazine is long, most will hold 6-8 rounds, and the damage is huge to whoever is on the receiving end of this blast. A shotgun, unlike a high-power rifle or pistol, delivers a big hole to the body of a bad dude, and if you use bird shot (7 ½ or 8s) it won't over penetrate walls and hurt innocent people in other parts of the house. Just the noise of your daughter pumping a shell into the chamber will send the worst of culprits fleeing.

Last But Not Least: Gun Safety and Storage

1. Always keep the gun pointed in a safe direction. This means always. Do you know what always means? If for some reason you're dazed and confused to the definition of always, here it is: every time; on every occasion; without exception. The "safe direction" is determined by, hello, the safest direction. You must, must keep the front of the barrel pointed away from anything you do not want to kill, at all times. Pay attention: Handling real guns is no game. There have been plenty of "unloaded" guns that have "accidentally" killed people who were just "playing around." Do you understand point one? If not, you should never own a gun.

2. Always keep your finger off the trigger until ready to shoot. When you are holding a gun, rest your finger on the trigger guard or along the side of the gun. You must practice not going to the trigger 100 times before you go to the range to shoot. You need to have this commandment drummed into your head. It must become a natural reaction when you pick up any kind of weapon. No "f-i-n-g-e-r on the t-r-i-g-g-e-r" 'til you're ready to fire in a safe direction. Period. It is pretty frickin' impossible for that gun to go off if the trigger is not pulled. Therefore, until you are actually ready to fire, do not even think about touching the trigger. Are we clear on this point?

3. Always keep the gun unloaded until ready to use. Whenever you pick up a gun, immediately engage the safety device if possible. Assume that the gun is loaded and treat it like it is loaded. If the gun has a magazine, remove it before opening the action and looking into the chamber(s) which should be clear of ammunition. If you do not know how to open the action or inspect the chamber(s), then put the gun down and leave it the heck alone and get help from someone who knows how to check it out. Is there anything about the above that you do not understand?

> *Store your guns so that kids and creeps can't get to them.*

Now that your girl is a gun owner she has massive responsibility slapped upon her shoulders, so...listen up. Most states impose some form of legal duty on adults to take reasonable steps to deny access by children to dangerous substances or instruments. Therefore, when her little siblings, nieces and nephews, or drunk buddies come over, make certain her fully loaded .44 magnum is not laying next to the remote control in her living room.

It is the individual gun owner's responsibility to understand and follow all laws regarding gun purchase, ownership, storage, transport, etc. Father/Daughter: If you do not know what you are legally required to do then contact your state police and/or local police for information regarding such laws. Remember, it's your ass if something bad happens.

Therefore, store your gun(s) so that kids and creeps can't get to them. Gun shops sell a crazy variety of safes, cases, and other security devices. While specific security measures may vary, you must, in every case, assess the exposure of the firearm and absolutely ensure that it is inaccessible to a child or an unauthorized user. You dig?

For more information on gun use, safety, and other responsible gun owner 411 log on to *www.NRA.org.*

Lastly, dad, think of the different headlines that would be written if our lovely coeds were armed when attacked. Instead of watching another horrific news feed about a beautiful girl found stuffed in a 55-gallon drum, we read about thug bad boy gone to meet his ticked off maker because the chick he picked on was armed and dangerous. That's the report I want to start seeing, hearing and reading about: the good girl lives and the bad guy dies.

Amen?

FOUR

Teach Your Daughter How to Sense Bullshit

"One of the most salient features of our culture is there is so much bullshit."

Harry G. Frankfurt,
Princeton Philosophy Professor —

How many of you have met the book smart 4.0 magna cum laude lady who, in regard to street smarts, is a magna dumb loopy chick? What about the poor honey who is neither book nor street smart? What a shame, eh? My goal for my girls is to own the twain. My wife and I push our daughters to academic excellence. We insist that they strain their brains so they won't sound like Paris Hilton when they open their mouth.

That being said, as much as I want my little rays of sunshine to have a high GPA (not that a jiffy GPA means squat anymore given the bogus bunk being taught in school). I want them to have an equal or higher level of street smarts: What some would call a sixth sense, an otherness, a discerning spirit, a fourth dimension or what I call a well-honed and greased Bullshit Detector (BSD).

Street smarts will give our girls the shrewdness to see through the veil of crap most guys, governments, gimmicks, gadgets, gurus and evil girlfriends live behind. Therefore, in this chapter I want to help you help your daughter whet her BSD and overcome any proclivity she has to becoming as sharp as a sack of prunes and assist her to discern that which is detrimental to her life even if it's all dressed up as the greatest thing in all the world.

Thugs, bad boys, greasy politicians, scum-sucking marketing leeches, PR mooks, agents, corporate America, late night infomercials, televangelists, used car salesmen, and mechanics all love the gullible girl who has a weak dung detector. Therefore father, one of the most important things you can ever do for your daughter is to help her become a shrewd and skeptical sassy sister who cannot be bamboozled by people, places, and ideas that seek to do her harm.

Defining the Defecation and the Defecator

You can call it bullshit or BS, bull crap, or the nicer sounding Latin term *"stercore tauri"* or simply, bull, bull roar, bull pucky, bovine scat, horse feathers, horse hockey, poppycock, cow dung, Barney Frank, bollocks, gobbledygook, gibberish, humbug, fisk, nonsense, evening news, tall tale, pseudo-intellectualism, propaganda, fiction, lie, bunkum, spin, or truthiness.

Whatever you want to call it, bullshit can be defined as:

Communications where reality and truthfulness aren't nearly as vital as the ability to manipulate the audience to get it to do whatever one wants done.

Wikipedia states that BS is:

All skewed, spun, knowingly dubious, carefully framed, pretentious, misleading or vacuous statements.

Examples of "bullshit" include sales/marketing pitches, public relations release, and demagogic or disingenuous pronouncements made by politicians or defense attorney presentations.

"Bullshit" does not necessarily have to be a complete fabrication; with only basic knowledge about a topic, bullshit is often used to make the audience believe that one knows far more about the topic by feigning total certainty or making probable predictions. It may also merely be "filler" or nonsense that, by virtue of its style or wording, gives the impression that it actually means something.

In popular explanations of philosophy, the word "bullshit" is used to denote utterances and speech acts which does not add to the meaning of the set of sentences uttered, but which is added purely to persuade interlocutors of the validity or importance of other utterances.

The accuracy of the information is irrelevant whilst "bullshitting"; whether true or false, "bullshit" is the intention to distort the information or to otherwise achieve a desirable outcome, making "bullshit" a close cousin to rhetoric as Plato conceived it.

I know what you're thinking...Who would of thunk people could get so technical in defining verbal dung?! Hailing from Texas and being an average student I can't wax verbose in explaining the intricacies and delicacies of BS, but I sure can tell when someone is full of it.

Even though I'm a simple guy who likes to keep it simple, let's check out the derivation of our scat-based word and how, when and where it wove its way into the American whoop and warp. Here's what I've found:

"Bull," meaning nonsense, dates from the 17th century (Concise Oxford Dictionary), whereas the term "bullshit" has popularly considered to have been first used in 1915 by Theodore Roosevelt when he saw an ugly bearded woman carrying a temperance sign. The earliest attestation mentioned by the Concise Oxford Dictionary is in fact T. S. Eliot, who between 1910 and 1916 wrote an early poem to which he gave the title "*The Triumph of Bullshit.*"

> We must prep our daughters to deal with lies, hype, and spin.

In American slang the term came into popular usage during World War II. The word "bull" itself may have derived from the Old French word "boul" meaning "fraud, deceit" (Oxford English Dictionary). As to earlier etymology the Oxford English Dictionary cites bull with the meaning "trivial, insincere, untruthful talk or writing, nonsense."

Helping Your Daughter Hone Her BSD

As your girl plows through life she is going to be hit in postmodern times with a tsunami of sewage coming from various institutes and people. I know...I know...it's cruel, it sucks, and it's a shame that our kids have officially missed out on the *Leave it to Beaver* scenario that most of us were fortunate enough to have lived through. It's no use crying about it. We must prep them for the lies, hype, and spin they are going to face in this SNAFU'ed USofA. We must make certain our girls can deftly navigate the crap-laden rapids of our culture's

BS-bloated bouillabaisse and come out of this thing smelling like a rose. A high performance, ultra sensitive BS Detector is a must-have weapon in your daughter's conquer the planet toolbox. And the sooner your girl can discern deception when it's being delivered to her, the better. Start 'em young!

To keep it simple, tell your daughter that her BS detector is essentially that little voice inside her head telling her to listen to the little voice inside her head. It's an internal salvific alarm alerting her to the fact she's in the process of being bamboozled. If she ignores this in-house salvo it will be to her own detriment. If she hones her BSD and listens to it when it starts kicking her upside the head, she'll be the wiser, safer, and richer for it.

> *All girls have a bullshit detector.*

Everybody has a BSD. Obviously, some folks have better ones than others. No matter where your girl currently is in her abilities to spot BS in all of its varied forms, if she will apply the following principles I guarantee her dates with morons, her purchases of stuff she doesn't need, and her gullibility in regard to the MSM's propaganda will diminish and she will take on a shrewd life-saving edge if she will do these three simple things:

1. Become a skeptic.

Our English word skeptic comes from the Greek word *skopos*, which means someone who scopes things out. She's got to become the dame who walks around the car and kicks the tires. Get your daughter to be cautiously thorough before she buys and believes anything that is pitched to her.

Whether it's a car or a cult or a current politician, train her to look under the hood a little bit more would 'cha pops? An easy exercise to increase her righteous doubts is to have her stand in front of a mirror with her arms crossed and one eyebrow raised, looking down her nose and say, "yeah, right" in a sarcastic tone. Have her do this about 100 times every morning before she's off to school. This'll get her properly pissy in no time.

Yes, brother, it is your job to make your daughter healthily suspicious. This doesn't mean that she turns into a chain-smoking, angry and apathetic cynic, who, as Dennis Miller says, is always as willing to believe the worst as long as it takes as little effort as possible. Your goal as goalie of your girl's life is to make her cautious. It doesn't mean she's paranoid; it doesn't mean she won't take risks. It just means that she's not afraid to objectively judge what gets tossed in her plate and critically analyze it before she dates it, buys it or votes for it.

> Your job is to make your daughter healthily suspicious.

I'm a big game hunter and I am very proud of it. One thing I've noticed about truly wild trophy animals is that they are extremely suspicious of everything that walks, crawls or flies. They look at every bush, constantly sniff the air, listen intently for anything that is out of sync with their neck of the woods, and if for some reason something is not right about what they see, hear, smell and feel, they haul butt into the next zip code. They don't pray about it. They don't call up their TBN prayer counselor. They don't email Dr. Phil and query him regarding what to do. They don't think to themselves, you know, I really shouldn't be so judgmental. They don't ask their younger, dumber furry friends what would Jesus do, they split. And it is this wary nature that has made them the biggest, baddest, longest living and most sought after beast in the field. Pause and meditate on that nugget for a while, señor and señorita.

Your goal as a dad is to have your daughters clip along at such a "trophy" level of awareness that they avoid the ubiquitous wastoids who seek to do them harm.

Here are several things your girl should be skeptical of . . .

Most of the stuff sold on TV at 2 AM. More than likely it will not do what it purports to do.

The diet shake she's being tempted to purchase. It will not help her lose the 190 pounds she needs to lose in 14 days. If she's that obese and she's only got two weeks to shed the pounds, only a chain saw will help. I don't recommend it though. Give yourself a year of eating less and exercising more. It's called work.

Televangelists. 99.9% of them are preening Nancy boys looking to fleece you.

Any guy between the ages of 14-89 who says he loves you. That's a code word for I'm very horny and will do whatever and say whatever for sex.

The 8 Minute Abs DVD. Forget about buying it. You can't sit on your butt for 10 years not exercising and expect to look like Cameron Diaz in 480 seconds.

Polygamist Cults. Before your young girl joins a polygamist cult in Tweedleyournutsack, Texas, have her Google it. In addition she might want to contact the FBI and inquire if they have any plans on raiding their el Rancho Apocalypto anytime soon. Just a suggestion.

2.   Trust your Gut.

God has hardwired us so that when we are in danger, or when we're getting scammed, or when we're about to say, "Yes, coffee sounds great!" to an axe murder that our body, mind, and spirit freak out. Our "gut" will check us and the little voice inside our head will start calling us unflattering names attempting to get our attention before we get raked over the coals. Remember, your gut check/BSD is your friend, and never forget this maxim: When you are picking up on something, you're picking up on something. Pay attention, por favor.

Check this out. Fifteen years ago my wife and I were given a vacation on a dude ranch in the Texas Hill Country. It was a spectacular place outside of Kerrville. We were afforded the opportunity to just chill, or hunt, or fish, or float down a river in a canoe or ride horses. My little girls loved horses, and being the sucker I am for their doe-eyed requests to ride horsies we saddled up and rode the trails and had a great time strolling through the countryside on horseback. It was a good day.

> *Listen to that little voice inside your head.*

That night as we were winding down for bed we were looking at the various things afforded to us at the ranch and our little girls wanted to ride the horses again. So me being the excellent father that I am, I said, cool...horses it is. And with that we went to sleep.

The next morning we woke up, had breakfast and then we went back to our cabin to get ready to saddle up. My little ladies were looking at me with excitement and love. I was the greatest dad in the world. We were having a blast. Then, all of a sudden, I got this weird feeling that we shouldn't go horseback riding. I couldn't shake that feeling. I was thinking, if I cancel the horses then I'm going to morph from Captain Fantastic to Mr. Jackass PDQ!

I couldn't figure out for the life of me why I was freaking out over going horseback riding. I thought, *am I a wussy?* Is this all about my childhood terror trip I had on my cousin's horse that attempted to kill me? Do I need some time on the couch? Some Xanax? What the heck is wrong with me?

Finally, the feeling was so great that I pulled my wife aside and told her, "babe, I don't think we should get on the horses . . ." She's asked, "why?" with that "what hell is wrong with you, you little hamster" look on her face. I responded, "I don't know, I just have this weird feeling." So, with that I told my girls we weren't going riding but fishing instead, and they gave me the predicted evil, daddy's-gone-crazy stare.

With my ticked off family in tow, we all started schlepping toward the pond to go fishing. I was walking with my oldest girl, who was four, and mi esposa was pushing our two-year-old in our stroller through the mud. Yep, the fishing trip was sucking already. As we were setting up to fish, all the pretty people on horseback started filing past us losers fishing on the banks of a stinking lake. We looked like idiots standing in the mud. The kids were giving me the stink eye, horse flies were eating up my wife, and there I was trying to be positive and con them into trying to be happy. The riders waved at us and then disappeared into the bush and up the mountain. My wife looked at me again with that you're-not-going-to-get-sex-for-the-next-ten-years look, and then it started to rain.

> My girls looked at me with jaw-dropping Moses-like awe, to which I replied, "Who's your daddy?"

We picked up all our crap and started heading back to our cabin when all of a sudden on top of the hill I saw horses without their riders running down into the valley. About five minutes later we saw the riders starting to walk down, some bleeding from the head, others holding their arms, some had to be carried out. We ran over there to see what had happened, and one of the riders said that when they got to the top of the hill one of the horses freaked out, tossed its rider and caused a chain reaction with the other horses throwing their mounts. My girls and I were listening to all this and then they turned and looked at me with jaw-dropping Moses-like awe, to which I replied, "Who's your daddy?"

What was that? It wasn't a phobia. It was just an inexplicable weird feeling I had that I could not shake. The bottom line with gut checks is if you're not an insane paranoid schizophrenic and for whatever reason you're not getting a sense of peace about a person, a place or a thing then your best bet is not to go there, girlfriend.

3. Hang out with mature, sharp and successful people and allow them to speak into your life.

I know for young people it's not sexy to hang out with people other than their peers. However, if you're honest, young lady, most of your girlfriends are dunces with very weak BSDs, correct? Now, I am in no way saying not to hang with your friends. Nor am I saying that because people are older they're smarter, because God knows there are a lot of old idiots cruising around this planet with seriously messed up lives who shouldn't be listened to anymore than you'd listen to a 19-year-old crackhead.

However, if your parents, grandparents, pastors or whoever are successful and have enriched, happy lives, sidle up to them because they can sharpen your BSD. They have expertise, experience, honesty, and a spiritual maturity that you can roll into your profit if you surround yourself with them...and if you listen.

Yes, señorita, you can become wise beyond your years, and by osmosis have a highly-attuned BSD which will set yourself up for safety and security by simply befriending and adhering to the counsel of mature, righteous adults. Yep, older folks who have been there and done that bring many things to the table that your goofy BFF cannot provide. Don't blow these people off. Matter of fact, the more you surround yourself with wise counselors the more life is going to kiss you on the mouth rather than kick you in the butt.

> Surround yourself with wise counsel and life will kiss you on the mouth rather than kick you in the butt.

One of the major perks that older, wiser, righteous relationships provide is that they'll point out your blind spots. Most of your friends have similar blind spots and weaknesses. That's why you hang out with them—because you have parallel likes, dislikes and demons! Y'know, the whole birds of a feather flock together stuff?

This usually is no big whoop until you bump up against some egregious BS that will hurt you and you don't have the support structure in your immature friends to point out to you that you're about to smack into a stone wall. Case in point: the ubiquitous Hollywood starlets who surround themselves with myopic mooks with similar maladies who don't point out to each other when one is being a daft jerk. Thus they are plagued with "bad luck." This could be easily cured by them hanging out and listening to a more mature group who have no qualms about telling them when they're being an ass and how they should live their life.

> *Someone who loves you will point out the flaws in your character.*

Someone who loves you and has your best interests in mind has no problem whatsoever showing you that part of your character or your decision-making processes that is poisonous of which you cannot see. Sure it might hurt your feelings as they lovingly expose your faux pas, but in the end you'll be safer and more successful than your willful friends who plow on with their stupidity, blind as a bat to their disastrous decisions.

That's one of the many things that I like about my wife. She takes care of my blind spots. If I have a booger hanging in my nose hairs that I can't see, she tells me. Or if I have a long nose hair, ear hair, something in my teeth, or I'm walking around with my pants unzipped, whatever I am unaware of she pulls me aside and says, "wipe your nose, zip up your pants, and cut those braidable nose hairs, okay Rapunzel?" I don't whine, file for divorce, tell her to quit judging me because I know she loves me and wants me to be respected and to look cool, so I listen to her in dealing with that which I cannot see. Do you, señorita, have that kind of person in your life who'll weigh in on your boyfriends, girlfriends, habits and choices? If not, say hello to disaster because it's coming if you're going to blow off your blind spots.

Seven Signs About Your "Boyfriend" That Should Set Your BSD to Screaming

The old adage says that love is blind and that marriage is an eye opener. Dad, have your girls tuck these things into her psyche (and into her bra) as helpful hints to avoid dating a dilatory dillweed and potentially marrying the man from hell. Ladies, you owe me for this one. Make your check out to "Doug Giles" and send it to PO Box

800554, Aventura, Florida, 33280. Put in the memo "he saved my backside." Here we go . . .

1. Does he expect you to get plastic surgery? Y'know, keeping one's self attractive for each other is one thing. Having a boyfriend suggest that you go under anesthesia and a flippin' scalpel because he prefers certain types of breasts, lips, nose or hips is quite another.

Girls, if that is what your man is hinting or outright demanding that you do, then you, my friend, have a moron in your midst and your BSD should be shattering your ear drum about now. Look, if I were a girl I wouldn't stick sacks of boat chalk (silicone) into my chest for anyone. If you wish to do it for whatever reason, so be it. But do not, under any circumstance, go under the knife for some tripod hooked on porn that's trying to get you to carve up your carcass in order to look like spankmeister's favorite online lady.

However, before you tell him to get lost, have some fun with him and tell him you'd prefer him to get some lipo, remove his third nipple, trim his Adam's apple a tad, get some micro mini grafts and a penis implant (or a substantial reduction). See how the Palm Pilot likes having the guns turned on his challenged areas.

2. Does he hang out with horndogs? If he's hanging out with guys who hate their wives, who love to indulge in the superfluity of naughtiness and who are out to convert the faithful to the Cult of Infidelity, that's a bad sign—if you like fidelity, that is. Be not deceived: His bad company will land him in a strip club or an illicit affair, and you'll end up crying on your pillow and stabbing his photograph.

3. Does he have a frickin' job? Ladies, you don't want a guy who does not work his butt off. I know feminism has sold you on being the breadwinner, but trust me, the "I'm in love" buzz will soon wear off if your boyfriend stays unemployed. Sure it will seem okay for a couple of months as he is "finding himself," but after a year of you bringing home the drachmas while he masturbates and watches Jerry Springer all day...well, trust me, that will get real, real, real, real old. Also, not only should he get a job, but he should be aggressively making certain that he is con-

stantly excelling at what he does and thereby securing for himself some serious flow.

4. Does your boy toy lead? I know, I know, metrosexual dev-ilish misandry has taught men to be the little princesses; however, God would like men to rise up and play the Spartan in the spiritual, physical and financial well-being of a relationship.

    If he shoves everything off onto you, the girlfriend, you got yourself a twinkie. And no girl worth her salt wants a twinkie. Tell him to pull his head out from his buttocks, shake the irresponsibility from his soul, reject passivity and now go be a courageous leader. If he does this con-sistently for the next, oh…let's say, ten years, then you can think about once again dating the dandy.

5. Does he fart at the dinner table? Girls what did Aretha Franklin teach you? What did she tell you through song? R-E-S-P-E-C-T that's what. If you don't respect yourself, he won't respect you either. Remember, Uncle Doug warned you.

6. Does he speak down to you? Does he speak to you as if you are an ignorant and deaf dromedary? If he does put Exlax in his chocolate chip cookies, set up a video camera in his bathroom, get the video after his diarrhea session, upload it on YouTube and then break up with him. Text him with the url link and say, "never, never talk down to me!"

7. Does he still speak to his old girlfriends? Do you really need me to explain this one further unto you?

FIVE

Teach Your Daughter How to Rebel

Dad, having a girl with a well-whetted BS detector is not enough to deter some thugs, especially belligerent bad boys with vapid values and a whacked worldview. Sometimes, when the twaddle gets egregious, we've got to teach our little darlings to revolt against its purveyors.

As you know, dad, for the last several decades there has been a belligerent, systematic secularization of the United States by the liberal thought police. These individuals have sought to remove from all public sectors of society any semblance of biblical values, all influence of religious institutions, all sacred symbolism and the traditional core values that have made America great. A Cyclops can see that.

Of the many mental illnesses the secularists suffer from, two primary pains motivate them to work against the universe: 1) a repulsion from God and 2) a massive American History memory loss.

Being saddled with these sicknesses, instead of seeking healing or having an exorcism or joining MA (Misguided Anonymous) or just moving their butts to Holland where they'll be nice and comfy, they have chosen, rather, to create a new United States of Sassy Secularists in which the traditionalist is kicked to the curb and their novel material girls get to govern.

To accomplish the creation of the USSS, they have become busy monkeys trying to level authorities, rewrite records, become judge and jury of all things everywhere, homogenize cultures, pimp style over substance and deify power while they prop up the "victims of the system" to drive their imagined American magic bus.

On Planet Secularity where "truth is dead," muscle-power becomes the operative standard of speech. The results are cultic conformity and group bullying. The chief orgasmic goal of the secular sellers of societal swill is to create a rock-solid environment of political correctness—with the intended end being the cowing of people who might rustle their feathers by not parroting their already tried (and been found wanting) opinions. They can't allow people to speak and think freely because the realist and the truth dealer would pee on their little party.

Therefore, the person who champions a traditional view of truth (not propaganda), who stands for the historical record (not the hysterical read) and who believes that biblically-based, previously proven and transcendent standards should continue to serve as an external pattern to govern our nation's character will endure more scorn than Ted Nugent, Rush Limbaugh and me crashing Rosie's "Lesbians Only" plus size pool party. (That was a very rough Dougified paraphrase from an Os Guinness speech. No offense, Os.).

However, the secularist's opposition to the traditionalist's values shouldn't rattle the righteous rebel dad and daughter. No, this brazen attack by bloviating boors should actually turn the upright dissenter on. The faithful traditionalist who loves God and the way this nation was originally constituted will joyfully stand up against this hijacking of our nation by the "progressive" Philistines. Yes, the grand and the noble girl will not lie down and roll up like an opossum just because the truth isn't en vogue. Great people side with truth even when it's detested.

> *Great people side with truth, even when it's detested.*

The traditionalist who is worth her salt will not put on Butt-Smacker lip balm and kiss the chunky backside of the secularists when they jam it in her face for an acquiescing smooch. No sir. No way. Not now. Not ever. Rather, the hardy traditionalist, while humming the words to Twisted Sister's hit song, *"We're Not Gonna Take It,"* will continue to speak out, work hard and self sacrifice in order to preserve classic traditional Judeo-Christian values.

As stated, we need, as in right now, not only men but women, pops, who hold to traditional values to become rebels with a cause. The problem is, however, most people with family values/faith have become too nice to fight in the public arena for God's grand principles.

Yes, somehow a large chunk of the church has embraced a feckless faith, lead by a cardigan wearing Nancy boy Jesus and have contented themselves with being tolerant doormats for dillweeds with dense ideas. I, on the other hand, don't play that game because, as I see it, I serve a great God whose principles are not to be compromised and are worth fighting for (and passing on), and I happen to sport a virulent west Texas "don't tread on me" spirit.

The reality is, pops, that our daughters have been birthed in the midst of a raging culture war where time-honored principles are being thrashed. The chances of our kids inheriting an America like we have been blessed with are about as likely as Kimora wearing the same panties seven days in a row.

> Don't drink the testicle-shrinking doctrine that says Jesus is a wussy!

No doubt some of you nicer fathers are having a hard time trying to square being a Christian, raising a polite and charming Christian daughter and at the same time encouraging her to be a righteous rabble-rouser against the secular thugs.

It could be because you have drunk the testicle shrinking poisonous doctrine brewed by secularists—namely that Jesus is one big wussy. As I blathered earlier, I believe a significant portion of the church has bought into the notion that if you're a Christian you're supposed to be accepting of whatever crap culture crams down your pie-hole. Could you be a gobbler of this toxic waste?

The secularists love to propagate their Boy George image of Christ to Christians, i.e., the sweet, could-be-gay, definitely cowed Jesus who is always accommodating and never dissenting, a veritable stained glass Gumby who'll bend when pressured.

Yep, the secularist tools joyfully tout this unbiblical, emasculated image of Immanuel to their ilk, and a lot of the church is stupid enough to gulp it down and ask for seconds. The thugs and the bad boys on the Left love it when Christians buy into this perversion of Jesus' person and work as it makes them squishy dolts that are easily controlled.

If, as fathers with traditional values, we want our daughter to have a fair to middling chance that the USA, which she and her kids will inherit, will bear some semblance of its former glory and greatness, then I believe (first and foremost) we have got to dispense with this candy cane Christ that we have been sold.

One way to do this, dad, is to grab a Bible, a highlighter, your daughter, a couple of beers, a nice cigar (I recommend the Tatuaje Havana VI Artistas - Torpedo) and go through the scripture and mark every counterculture and confrontational thing Christ did when he cruised this planet. The pages will quickly turn fluorescent yellow, and you will swiftly be blown away by the ubiquitous examples of Jesus' "unChrist-like" behavior. After you blow through the gospels with your girl reading with a special eye toward the rebel texts then do this, dad:

Sit back and relax. Drink in what you just read.

Take a deep sip of your ice cold Corona,

Draw a huge hit off your stogie, and then

Apologize to your daughter for ever thinking and maybe even teaching the heretical concept that Jesus was a cliché-doling bearded lady, and lastly . . .

Let the power of the scripture and the Holy Spirit purge forever the notion from your soul that Jesus was a twinkie who put up with political, cultural and ecclesiastical nonsense.

> Read the Bible to your daughter, outlining every rebel thing Jesus did.

Yes, dad you read me right; it has got to be you that does this. Not your wife. Not granny. Not Pastor Dudley Paunch-Gut whose masculinity is seriously in question, but you. You have to lead the spiritual charge with your daughter. Not just mom but you too, dude. Why? Well, primarily it is because men bring the testosterone-laden rebel fog to the text, and this holy testicular attitude is what your righteous daughter needs if she is going to survive society's toxicity.

For example: Here's what I, the proud President of The Testosterone Fog Club, get when I read about Christ in the gospels and the book of Revelation, and this is what I bring to my little Bible "studies" with my ladies:

When Jesus Christ got injected into the human mix two thousand plus years ago, from the cradle to the cross, He was a lightning rod of controversy. His incarnation heated up the culture war more than

O'Reilly could ever dream of doing.

> Your daughter needs your holy, testicular-laden attitude to survive society's toxicity.

Immanuel's arrival upon the scene caused demon-inspired political idiots to try to kill Him while He was still cooing and pooing in His pampers. The dragon no likey his party getting ruined, and ruin it the Prince of Peace did.

The initial message the Wonderful Counselor preached, according to Dr. Luke's take, ticked off the crowd He was addressing so thoroughly that they attempted to throw Him off a cliff. He nailed that haughty mob for the crud they were practicing—and He did so publicly. In public. Ouch. Snap! That's not very "Christian" of Christ!

In reality (on this planet), Jesus received minimal accolades. No lucrative gigs with the Premier Speakers Bureau; no "Isn't He so nice! Let's put Him on Oprah" invite; no fat, Creflo Dollar-like honorariums; no limousine chariot services. He got nada, nothing, zilch, zero, zippo—and for those who haven't seen *The Passion of the Christ* yet, it sorta got even rougher.

The truth of the matter is that what Jesus said and did caused more discomfort to man's me-monkey human spirit than cheap tequila and three bags of pork rinds drenched in hot sauce would to Rachel Ray's colon. I make it clear to my girls that today, in our radically wussified, politically correct state of bland, our culture wouldn't embrace the Christ of Scripture because He'd get under our skin. And we love our skin.

Understanding the importance of a dad's spiritual input into their daughter's life is pretty easy. The simple math is...dads bring the balls to the Bible and like I said...girls need the chutzpah those under the influence of testosterone bring to the scripture and to their spiritual life, that is, if they are going to rise up to the challenges of our mucked up 21st century.

> The simple math is dads bring the balls to the Bible.

Think about it: When men, who are unashamed of being hairy, burping, farting, scratching and competitive creatures, read the scripture they don't see kitty cats and candy canes. They see life and death, heaven and hell, amazing grace and eternal damnation, wicked demons and fierce angels in the context of a spiritual war that's headed up by an unconquerable Christ. Yes sirree bob dog, they do not read the Bible through the perverted spectacles of Precious Moments sunglasses. They read the Word through a testosterone fog, a thick primal haze created by the King of Kings of which he said...it is good!

Obviously, I believe one of the reasons traditionalists have spawned capitulating softies is because the dads with the 'nads have ducked out of the spiritual equation of his kids. Yes, the chances are extremely high that if his input is absent or lacking that his kids' spirituality will take on an imbalanced, effeminate quality and will be minus the rowdy rebel funk that men bring to the table and will therefore be a non-resistant Britney to an addle-pate's bad idea.

> *Jesus didn't act nice all the time and neither should you.*

From my admittedly imbalanced and demented mind that is always way too cranked up on the juice, I'm convinced that the Christian father of a daughter will by fiat make her a staunch combatant for traditional/Christian values—just as their Savior was. Yep, I'm sold on the precept that if one truly follows Jesus that they not only will be graceful to the sinful but will also be antagonistic to idiots who won't break with their idiocy, especially when the bad ideas detrimentally affect multitudes.

So, traditionalist, teach your daughter to be nice, to mind her own business, to help old ladies across the street, but realize that you and your little girl are alive in the midst of a raging culture war. You must realize that Jesus wasn't nice all the time and neither should you be, especially when His standards today are getting the same treatment that a fire hydrant gets from a dog.

Where and How to Raze a Little Hell

Having hopefully persuaded the God- and country-loving father of the flappdoodle their daughters are growing up in and the inability for them to hide behind Christ and Christianity to avoid confronting this craziness, I now give thee and thine my two cents on where rebellion will be most necessary and how your daughter can go about raising an effective stink.

The chief point of assault upon your little chica is going to be via government schools, as the secularist's have officially hijacked these

institutes and have turned them into the main source of their misin-
formation indoctrination. This will be the first major battle field in
her life. If she survives this fray with her
Judeo-Christian values intact, she'll be one
heck of a warrior for the rest of her life.

> Teach your daughter to believe in God and to not have her genitals turned into a campus Jiffy Lube.

Hear me well, dad: If you're going to
send your cupcake to a public school or a
state run university, then you've got to teach
your lass not to just sit there in class being a
good girl and taking whatever propaganda
the secular "progressives" shove down her
throat. You must teach her to deftly defy defunct dogmas and not turn
a blonde eye to bad ideas.

Yes, traditional father, you've got to teach your mademoiselle to feel
proud and comfortable with not being a communist, with believing
in God, with our nation's spiritual heritage and with not having her
genitals turned into a campus Jiffy Lube. At today's universities, your
college student will be a radical if she doesn't lock step to the secularization, slutification and wussification that these institutions and their
devotees try to cram up her and America's orifices. Turn her into a
21st century finger-flying secularist-defying Rosa Parks for that which
is holy, just, and good.

If your daughter has been somewhat sheltered in home school or
via a Christian school and then she gets dumped into a state run university, she's going to be more shocked than Khalid Sheik Mohammed
at a Jay Alexander pool party. Yes, within the first couple of weeks of
entering college she's going to have her liberal campus and its profes-
sors shove more junk down her throat than
Rosie does her gullet during Chili's Monday
Night Nacho Monster Blowout Special.

Is she ready?

Now, I'm not trying to make you fearful,
father. I just want you and yours to brace for
the liberal Kool-Aid crunch that is coming

> Turn your daughter into a finger-flying, secularist-defying Rosa Parks!

soon to a classroom near you. The stuff O'Reilly has warned you about
is true. The reality is, dad, that your daughter is entering the Liberal's
madrasah. Your/Her values, for the next four years, will be violated
much like Linsday Lohan's nose, liver, Mercedes and panties have been

for the last five years.

Given this milieu, the traditionalist señorita has essentially three options to choose from when confronted with the liberal hooey. The options are:

1. She can drink the campus Kool Aid and do the Dhimmocratic do-si-do.

2. She can run from the conflict to a likeminded conservative ghetto group and hide on the curb with the little cowering crowd.

3. She and her concurring buddies can get prepped and be a conservative crew that enters campus life and joyfully, earnestly and courageously challenges the purveyors of anti-American propaganda.

Door number three, as far as I'm concerned, is the only righteous choice. As I was entering my university years, I was (and still am) a kick butt and take names type of guy. Absorption and separation were not options for me (still aren't). I wanted to change things when I was at school, and I had a blast mixing it up on my campus back in the day, which, by the way, has paved the way for a pretty cool life. Excuse me while I relish in the fruits of my labor.

Okay, I'm back.

Look, given the slop the US is currently saddled with, if your daughter has an inkling of concern for her country, then an informed, entertaining and incendiary infiltration of her institute is the only answer. (How's that for alliteration?) Isn't that what college and youth are all about, namely, rebellion? Isn't teenage angst all about hell raising—or in our case, hell razing? C'mon, girlfriend...don't you want to get rowdy?

The Conservative/traditionalist is the rebel of our day. Yes, the times they are a changin' (have changed). "The Man" and "The Machine" on campus to rage against is not stodgy traditionalism, but rank secularism and its moral and political vacuity. Meet the new boss—it's not the same as the old boss.

For those new students who wish to make a dent on their campus, not only for their sake but for the following generations, I have nine things your girl must get if she wants to absolutely screw with the asinine screwballs at her university. To be an effective agent of change have her do the following:

1. **Get a sense of humor.** Most liberal profs and student activists are a screeching, nerve-grating, nasaly bunch of whiners. As a matter of fact, I'd rather watch Janet Reno do jumping jacks and hack squats in Borat's thong than listen to the hemp-clothed, goatee-bearing, chunky liberal bleat.

    Therefore, conservative student, when you queue up to address your crowd, be pleasant, poke fun at yourself, remove the whine from your voice and use honed humor to humiliate the Left. Getting folks to laugh at your opponents and not being rabid about taking yourself so seriously helps get your point across. To upgrade your general funniness, get Judy Carter's book, *Stand Up Comedy*.

2. **Get creative.** God bless technology. Conservative rebels, you have at your fingertips the wherewithal to go creatively crazy for the cause of God and country with the real possibility of a stack of people seeing and hearing what you have to offer.

    Therefore, get nutty with your stuff. Utilize these amazing techno tools to tackle the tools on the left. Take your gift, your talent, your voice and your God-wired weirdness and, every now and then, put something artistic out there that'll overtly or covertly slam dance the secularists who seek to sabotage our society. To upgrade your competitive creativity get *Chasing Cool*, by Noah Kerner and Gene Pressman.

3. **Get tough.** One thing that drives me nuts about some Sallys on the right is their bemoaning how they get attacked when they go public in the classroom with their sentiments. Whaa! What did you think the Ward Churchills were going to do, clap? Buy you candy? Wash your undercarriage? Look, not-so-sharp holder of tra-

ditional values, we're in a very real culture war. The crap will hit the fan when you counter the liberal crud in the classroom. Embrace it. Suck it up. Get tough. Let adversity be your Wheaties, the breakfast of champions! If you want to upgrade your resiliency, get my book, *The Bulldog Attitude: Get It or Get Left Behind.*

4. **Get prayerful.** Most folks on the ludicrous left who embrace what 21st century Dhimmocrats currently spew are admitted atheists. Seeing that they don't believe in the God who is, I'm a-guessin' they are probably not down the funnel with the discipline of prayer. That is, until they're about to die. Then, of course, they start praying like Chris Tucker freshly filled with the Holy Ghost and fire. Since they refuse to believe and pray to God, they have no supernatural help in their hapless cause. At least no positive supernatural help because we all know demons love to assist these guys. But I digress...

   The traditionalist (usually) believes in the God of Scripture...the God who's got a will and way that He'd like to see implemented on the planet. This is cool; however, God follower, take it to the next level and start praying with faith and oomph for His will to be done on earth as it is in heaven (this includes your campus).

   So...God-fearing traditionalist, ask God for *a)* crazy clout to change yourself so that you're not a waste-oid He's got to work around and *b)* for a dynamic enabling to effect constructive change on your campus and culture. To upgrade your prayer life, get E. M. Bounds' classic, *Power Through Prayer.*

5. **Get informed.** Conservative contrarians, you've got to get the following books and read them:

   The Politically Incorrect Guide to American History

   The Politically Incorrect Guide to Darwinism and Intelligent Design

   The Politically Incorrect Guide to English and American Literature

The Politically Incorrect Guide to Global Warming and Environmentalism

The Politically Incorrect Guide to Islam (and the Crusades)

The Politically Incorrect Guide to Science

The Politically Incorrect Guide to the Constitution

The Politically Incorrect Guide to the South (and Why It Will Rise Again)

The Politically Incorrect Guide to Women, Sex, and Feminism

Digest the above and when appropriate, take some of the factoids found within these secularism-devastating tomes and share them with your prof during class and your buddies in the dorm. It's fun for the whole family.

6. **Get speakers to your campus who'll fire up your base.** Young America's Foundation has an entire smorgasbord of world-class speakers covering every conceivable topic who can deftly dismember the left's bereft beliefs. To upgrade your campus base, go to *YAF.org*, order one of their ideological black belts and let the party start. In addition, you can book me to speak to your group. I'd love to come and toss the cat among the pigeons. Go to *ClashRadio.com/ seminars*, and let's yuck it up!

7. **Get sharp looking.** Most campus Liberals have a monopoly on ugly. They are neither pleasing to the ear nor eye. Do not follow their lead, young conservative. If they want to look sloven, unshorn and tie-dyed, let 'em. You, however, should run in the opposite direction.

    Don't believe that smack about looks don't matter. The heck they don't. If I have the choice between these two options: *1)* to look at and listen to an obese girl with frizzed out hair and so many piercings that it looks like a tackle box blew up in her face while she's wearing no bra with her 40DDD floppies staring right at me while she is yelling or *2)* to look at and listen to a svelte, well put together, conscientious lass graciously appealing to me, I am telling you right here and now that I'll choose #2. The nasty girl has offended my senses, lost my attention, and I could not care less what she has to say. Call me crazy. Girls, to upgrade your appearance, get *A Guide to Elegance: For Every Woman Who Wants to Be Well and Properly Dressed on All Occasions*, by Genevieve Antoine Dariaux.

8. **Get your grades up.**

9. **Get your hands dirty.** Serve your campus and community. The world has enough of derisive, hate-filled protests and marches by ideological miscreants. While you're in college, help in the critical areas of your campus and community's needs and watch the campus and community give you a standing O.

The Use of Comedy in Rebellion

I feel like I wouldn't do the traditionalist girl with conservative values justice if I didn't spotlight an effective tool of revolt, namely comedy. I know I'm not supposed to say this as a conservative and as a Christian, but Steve Colbert, Jon Stewart, and David Letterman are funny hombres. Even though I radically and fundamentally disagree with most of their content, funny is as funny does. They're like farts. Most folks don't really like farts, but farts are funny. Period. Especially, when it's yours and it's silent.

Look, as far as comedy goes, Miss Conservative, you must bow and kiss the Left's ring. They slay us. And because they slay us both in sheer number of comedians and in comedic talent they are currently a massive asset for the secularists in their revolt against traditional America. You can count on one hand how many conservatives are making a semi-distinct blip on the comedic scene. Who do we have? Dennis Miller, Brad Stine, and Julie Gorin.

> *Steve Colbert, Jon Stewart, and David Letterman are funny hombres. They're like farts.*

Why can't conservatives get their comedic act together? The liberals, on a 24/7 basis, are tossing us soft balls that we should be driving out of the park in a humorous, prime time, way. It's so easy it's stupid. All we have to do is just read the crap that the left does out loud, and it's hilarious. We don't even have to be that imaginative and try to develop quips, as they provide an endless supply of ammunition. We couldn't make up the stuff they do even if we wanted to—no one on the planet is that creative.

> *Conservatives are not funny, because we've become nicer than Christ.*

The secular left is an amalgam of mayhem, a veritable *Star Wars* bar scene, a rogue gallery of freaks, geeks, nuts, sluts, slick politcos and skanky hos—and we're letting them walk without skewering the living daylights out of them.

What's wrong with us? We've become nicer than Christ.

From Hollywood to the Hill, the Left and those who lean that way do more psychotic stuff than my one-eyed Uncle Joe does on a three day weekend binge when he's all liquored up. They are a MadTV, SNL and HBO Special waiting to happen. There has to be some conservative capital lying around that can be earmarked to gather no-holds-barred comedians to paper shred these little darlings on TV and in film.

So why don't conservatives crank out comedians? Here's why I think our comedic contributions are weak.

1. **Conservatives, obviously, don't think comedy is important.**

The Daily Show and *The Colbert Report* don't have *The Factor* numbers. Thus, they don't seem to be as important as O'Reilly, or Rush or Hannity in an immediate sense. And they're not. However, Steve and John do have the ear of millions of 18-35 year olds, who will, uh... hello, be at the wheel driving this nation a few short years from now. That's kinda significant.

The Right is foolish and stupid not to be knocking themselves out to compete for the belly laughs of this demographic. Blowing off this bunch that's not listening to conservative talk radio, watching Bill, or logging on to *TownHall.com* is to diss a crowd that will, in short order, be influencing our nation after you take the big dirt nap, conservative mom and dad.

Conservatives have got to get their ideas to the masses in modes other than talk radio, online newsportals, and Fox News. If conservatives want to do more than choir preach and want to get their message to the young masses, then comedy and satire must come to the forefront.

2.   We spit out lame comedians.

When it comes to conservatives and Christians doing comedy, like soup in a bad restaurant, their brains are better left unstirred. Conservative comedians, especially Christian comedians, are not that funny. The reason why? Well, I think they're too nice. They don't really set the hook. They don't really deliver the dig. For some reason, the laughmeisters of the Right are PC addled. Fear of negative press has gripped most of our funny men and women. When one is worried about what others will think they cannot really queue up to deliver a scorching and hilarious screed aimed at deflating whoever they're after. Political correctness kills the comedian's ability to say what needs to be said and how they need to say it. If conservatives want to compete comically they're going to have to get raw. I'm talkin' gloves off UFC slugfest funny.

> *Political correctness kills the comedian's ability to say what needs to be said.*

3   We're too serious.

With our war with whacked out Islam and our ideological battle with the Secularists who whiz on traditional American values, the conservative can become a sober and somber person, which is understandable.

That doesn't mean we can't laugh, or more specifically, mock our enemies. Satire, comedy and laughter are great stress relievers and confidence builders. It's a show of strength. It's a sign that you're ready to play. Nowadays, we won't dare draw cartoons about Osama and his ilk lest we tick them off. Are you kidding me? We're trying to kill the terrorists, right? Let me see if I get this correct: We can kill them, but we can't insult them with cartoons or sitcoms?

In regard to the secularists and their jacked-up notions of where they'd like to take America, when the killer conservative comedians come forth and deftly employ their craft, I believe they will sway, through the rebel laughter, tens of thousands of ideological fence strad-dlers who are just waiting for us to get more hip and lighten up a bit.

> We can kill terrorists, but we can't insult them with com-edy? What's up wth that?

Comedy is a tool of derision that is impor-tant if you want to start and fuel a revolution. The conservative girl worth her salt has got to champion and use comedy against the secu-larist tools on the left. Look, it's not enough just to sit back and moan about the things we don't like. We've got to go the extra mile and have fun at their expense... all the while tabling, in an entertaining way, what we believe will uphold this great land and that for which it stands.

One of the reasons why some young people no likey conservatives is because no one is making them look at the Left and then laugh their butts off at them. It seems shallow, but that's reality. I believe we need to change this by going Monty Python nuts. I'm willing to give it a try. My wife says I'm pretty funny, especially during sex. I'm not quite sure what she means, though.

With a Rebel Yell, She Cried "More, More, More!"

Lastly and seriously ladies, if America continues to: diss God, follow cultural coarsening Snookies, whiz on traditional values, weaken in our chutzpah, stop spitting out babies and continues to say "muy bien" to this insane illegal immigration invasion, then as a super power we will be in more trouble than a naïve, giggly good-looking drunk girl, or guy, at a Dennis Rodman keg party. We will be toast. Period. End of story. The universe will be against us, and we don't want to tick the universe off.

No civilization has lasted long as King of the Hill when there was a death of faith, a degeneration of morals, contempt for traditional values, a collapse of culture, a paralysis of the will, a decline in its native born population, and foreign invasion that wasn't resisted. Google it if you don't believe me, as the aforementioned is well known 411 regarding na-tions that have Gary Busey-ed their being into cheesy tourist spots.

Hey American girl...we're not invincible. I know it looks like it, but believe it or not there have been powerful civilizations that are now a cartoon of what they used to be, and it would be the height of hubris to think that this party will never end no matter what we do.

Look folks, here's the deal, if we forego the foundations upon which our country was built and start winging it with "progressive" principles instead of our old school traditional values, substituting God's eternal blueprint for some secularist wizard's ideas for a better mañana, then we officially put ourselves in line for an historical butt kicking. And we have plenty of enemies hoping that we will blissfully blow off the very nitty-gritty that got us to this place of global greatness. Fo' shizzle my nizzle.

I think God, in his crazy patience, is giving Americans (at least those who still give a flip about our country) a brief window to cowboy up and go back to the basics. If we do—great. I believe that with a lot of rebel work we can still salvage this thing. If we don't...then we shouldn't gripe when we see our motherland turn into tripe.

> *If we forego God's eternal blueprint, then we set ourselves up for an historical butt kicking.*

In addition, I believe young people who embrace traditional values are principle players in this momentary stay of execution.

So what can the young God- and country-loving person do? Well, you (and 48 year old guys like me) can do the opposite of what the secularist weeds want us to do, namely:

1. Embrace our faith like never before.

2. Cheer on traditional values.

3. Applaud and own our culture.

4. Quit being squishy wusses and steel up our will.

5. Spit out babies and raise them with a rock solid Judeo-Christian worldview.

6. Tell foreign invaders to come here correctly or go back to their sucky countries.

7. Revolt against the immoral vomit.

SIX

Teach Your Daughter How to be Classy

I'm ready to begin a Charlie Bronson vigilante campaign against male teenage hoodlums that terrorize their families, our neighborhoods, our schools and especially, our daughters. How I would love to shatter the knee caps, prune the tongues and staple the lips of these uber rude, demonic kids I see disrespecting our girls, their parents, and our elders with impunity.

I'm just kidding about hurting them. Well, not really.

Actually, I'm very serious about becoming a Billy Jack against such belligerent jerks, but the whole "against the law" thing keeps me from going Mach2 on these twisted monkeys.

What the heck has happened to kids today? These zit-faced, feckless zombies have zero etiquette, honor, respect, manners or sense of decorum for anything and anyone. Nothing is sacred to these idiots. Such irreverent inerts will destroy our country more radically and quickly than al-Qaeda could ever al-Hope to.

Not only are postmodern, tactless male teens gleefully gross and stupid but they perform all their demonic deeds with their pants hanging down below their chunky rear, and we have to stare at their butt cleavage as they clobber our culture.

To add insult to injury, we, the hard working, God- and country-loving taxpayers have to cover the insane costs these feral hogs create. The world would be better off without such oxygen thieves. I know it's tight, but it's right.

Girls can be just as bad. Thanks to Stupid TV women have officially been licensed to act like the basest of boys. Reality TV and our SNAFU'ed media have propped up girls, who are, from a classically classy standpoint, the antithesis of femininity. Yes, Hollywood lauds the shallow, privileged, repulsive, nerve-grating, brutish, sex-crazed and demanding ditz as a blueprint for girls everywhere. Run away from this image, my little darlings. Run away if you want to survive.

> *Thanks to Stupid TV women are licensed to act like the basest of boys.*

Sure some of the females Tinseltown vomits up might have talent, but the majority that the media tables for our chat stew are simply tawdry. The girls our culture ogles, by and large, are females but not ladies, in the classical sense of the word. They might have the right plumbing but they're more of a bigger breasted cartoon of Larry the Cable Guy versus a caring and gracious lady. They are nothing more than text messaging, spoiled, narcissistic hyenas who have figured out the power of their cash, their surname, a fresh scandal, being rude and the scepter their vajayjay sways. Girls, you should both pity and eschew such critters if you want to become a lady.

Indeed, ladies and gentlemen, if we were to remove the cash, the camera, their internet porn site, their daddy's last name and extract the double D silicone sacks from the chests of such pop fiction femmes they would be nothing more than Jerry Springer trailer trash on their way to living la vida broka. The only televised attention they would get would be on Cops when Officer Dudley Dipstick of the Tallahassee PD busts up the meth lab their first cousin/boyfriend is running. Git-R-Done girls.

And a big FYI to all young ladies who think being this kind of gross and slutty girl is cool: No true gentleman likes you, and you won't capture a quality guy. More than likely, unless Christ, Moses, Buddha or Tony Robbins rescues you, you'll end up a wrinkled and old multi-divorced dame who still goes to rock concerts when you're sixty, has a house full of cats, chain smokes Camels and yells at the contestants on the *Price is Right*.

Sadly, the only way some of these Legion-possessed undomesticated adolescents will leave their putrid path is by becoming the prison bride of a big dude in jail, catching a vicious STD, absorbing hot lead from a cop's Glock, or via a Damascus Road experience.

Since I, personally, cannot go Old Testament on these creatures of instinct without being thrown into the same prison to which they're headed, I have determined to be more positive and offer a more Oprah-like solution to our societal pollution.

> *Act like a gross and slutty girl and no true gentleman will like you.*

Yes, I've decided to turn to you, the dad, and give you some guidance in rearing that little bambina God has blessed you with and thereby help you help her not to become one of "them" who whizzes upon our national parade. I've got to warn you, my brethren, that if you omit these foundational lessons in decorum your kid will probably try to stab you in your sleep for not getting her the new Katy Perry CD she asked for. Be afraid.

The principles of etiquette I'm about to volley into your court are not new or original. They have been a part of the South and its heritage for many years, and their roots are biblical. Herewith is my ripped-off version of the recipe I got from Clint Johnson, the author of *The Politically Incorrect Guide to the South*, who probably got it from Emily Post, who got it from whomever, on how to raise lovely ladies who are classy rather than repulsive.

Follow this formula, father, and I guarantee she will steer clear of the local teen dumb crowd. Yes, if your girl is raised with reverence for what's holy, respect for our time-honored values and others I guarantee she will not give some tactless, tasteless thug the time of day. Unless, of course, it is to pray for him that he gets saved and delivered from being a total tool that's tooling his way to Dante's hibachi.

Herewith, compadres, are the 10 Commandments for Classy Chicas.

1. Don't flaunt your advantages.

The Classy Chica doesn't show off who she is, where she went to school or her net worth. Yeah, the bells and smells, the incense and nonsense afforded by certain advantages (earned or otherwise) don't mean a thing to a Classy Chica if used as a fig leaf to veil one's utter lack of character and humility.

Let me make it simple for you, dad and daughter: Everything that Paris Hilton, Britney, Omarosa, Lindsay, and New York (from Flavor of Love) does, do the opposite, and you will be a very pleasant and delightful young lady not hiding behind daddy's cash, mere talent, a Bose voice processor or fifteen minutes of fame.

> *Classy girls do the opposite of Paris, Lindsay and Britney.*

A girl with class, unlike Paris, Britney, and Lindsay, understands with all the external trappings of success and achievement she can still be a cultural pain in the butt and a horrible person. Therefore, focus not upon dusting up the transient trappings that dazzle the ubiquitous morons but rather pursue the hidden qualities of internal virtues that truly make a girl great, at least in God's eyes. Be known principally for being a good person and not for the stuff you have. Hear me loud and clear: advantages/talent without virtue = a train wreck.

2. Everyone deserves respect until they demonstrate they don't deserve it.

The Classy Chica believes that all people are created in the image of God and should be treated with respect until that person shows they don't deserve it.

That means they don't slap, spit or drop the F-bomb on their pastors, elders, teachers or parents. I asked Ted Nugent one time what he would do if one of his sons or daughters told him to F-off like Kelly and Jack Osborne regularly tell Ozzy and Sharon to do. Ted said, "I'd tear off their head and s#%t down their throat."

It's amazing to watch 3, 5 and 15 year-old kids unleash their venom on their parents and others and then walk away smacking their gum.

3. Titles are important.

The Classy Chica still calls their elders "sir" or "ma'am." I've got friends who have adult children with families of their own who make a very nice living, are close to my age and still call me "sir." When the Classy Chica addresses a man, it is always as "Mr. (last name)" and a woman as "Mrs." or "Miss (last name)" until they've been green lighted to use their first name or nickname.

4. Everyone else matters before you do.

The Classy Chica is here to serve, not be served. She does weird stuff like what needs to be done versus being some diva that expects everyone to wait on her. She doesn't rush an elevator knocking down granny to get on first. When she comes into a situation she assesses what others might need, not what she can get from people or places.

5. Be helpful.

The Classy Chica sees a need, and if she can assist then she helps. The other day I was out in front of a Publix Supermarket and watched a burglary in progress. The guy ran out of the store, cash in hand, with the clerk and security guards chasing him. It looked fun, so I joined in the chase. The clerk and the guard ran out of juice, and I (along with a cop) got to tackle the dude and jam his face into the cement. (One of those little perks God drops in your lap every now and then.) Bottom line with those raised as a Classy Chica is: Whether it's with tackling a punk or packing a trunk, The Classy Chica is programmed to H-E-L-P not hinder.

6. Be friendly.

The Classy Chica smiles. She's not sullen or vexed. She's not walking around like the psycho chicks and metrosexual males in Miami in a pout pretending to be the next angry supermodel. The Classy Chica says hello and starts friendly conversations. When I take my buddies hunting with me to Texas or Alabama, they're blown away at how friendly people are. We'll be driving down a Farm to Market Road in the middle of nowhere, meet a truck coming the opposite direction and our host will wave. Invariably, one of my friends then asks, "Who was that?" and our host replies, "I don't know." Then my jaded friends give me a confused look and ask me quietly why he waved. I whisper back, "People down here are friendly.... watch out—it might rub off on you."

7. Use the right words.

When asked a question, the Classy Chica doesn't reply with "Huh?" "What?" or "Yeah." It's "Please," "Thank you" or "Yes or no thank you." They are girls who respectfully ask and don't demand.

8. Don't dress like a skank.

There's nothing wrong with a girl dressing in a cute and figure-flattering manner. However, if you want to avoid drooling male troglodytes and be taken seriously as both a human and a woman then you must avoid wearing stripper heels to church. Send a message to the men out there by the way you dress that you're sophisticated and eloquent, not sleazy and easy, capisce?

9. Don't take nude photos of yourself or make sex tapes.

Unless you want a life in the porn industry with all the "perks" of drugs, STDs, crime and masturbatory stalkers/rapists, I'd really think twice about what kind of pictures and videos you have floating around on the internet. Lately, we have seen many aspiring young ladies have their careers derailed or their image forever slutified by the bad, bad decision of bumping uglies on film. Remember, not only is the paper patient, but so is the picture and the grainy home sex movie. These things can damage you for a long, long, long time.

10. Learn some cell phone etiquette.

First off, put your cell phone on vibrate, alright? There's enough noise pollution in our world without us having to hear your Razor blast out Nelly Furtado at ear-splitting decibels. Secondly, quit yelling on your phone. Just because you can't hear yourself in your cell phone's earpiece doesn't mean the caller can't hear you. In addition, by speaking softly we won't know how shallow and crazy you really are. Thirdly, if you're going to go nuts on the phone will you walk outside, huh? Fourthly, turn it off during church, okay Jezebel? Fifthly, if you won't text while we're eating dinner then I won't fart at the supper table, deal?

Father, disallow your child to act like a spoiled, rabid, egocentric animal. Make good manners and propriety a given for your girl, and I guarantee she will not attract the crotch-grabbing thugs amongst us. Instill the above Southern qualities into your baby, and when she grows up, she'll thank you in spades—and she'll be a respected, almost revered, leader wherever she goes.

SEVEN

Teach Your Daughter How to be a Visionary

One of the reasons why girls get involved with radioactive idiots is simply because they don't have squat going on in their lives. Goofy guys, to whom a sane girl wouldn't give the time of day (if she were focused and busy), find a window into a girl's soul when the little lady is big time lost in life.

Yep, a lot of talented, sweet, lovely, and educated girls get involved with buttheads simply because they're cosmically bored and have yet to dig deep into their psyche and find something great to live and die for. Thus they fill their soul's black hole with some male A-hole thinking, he...he...is what I really need!

Here's where you got to pray, pops, that the penny drops on her and she wakes the hell up to what heaven has for her because only getting a vision will wrest her from some Goober's arms for good.

Yes, father, the surest way to make certain that your niña doesn't take a shinin' to Johnny la Numb Nuts is to pray to God that she quickly gets the 411 for her l-i-f-e. An internal vision will negate negative people and habits in your little honey's life more than external rules and regulations ever could.

For example: Remember, dad, when you were a kid in high school? You were a dorky, gangly, snaggle-toothed, booger pickin', butt scratching, illiterate dill weed who put the funk in dysfunction. You didn't have a clue. Your existence gave overwhelming credence to Darwin's theory that you're a derivation from a stinkin' monkey rather than a clever creature crafted by an intelligent Creator.

C'mon pops, think back to when you didn't bathe, comb your hair, brush your teeth, wiped your nose on your sleeve, chewed with your mouth open, and cut farts at the dinner table so big and loud that they shook the very foundation of your house. Nothing could stop you from being the monosyllabic, slobbering, foul troglodyte that you were. Mama couldn't do it. Daddy couldn't do it. All of your teacher's, youth pastor's, and guidance counselor's combined efforts to alter you were all in vain.

What, my friend, caused you to get your act together? What made you morph from a stupid and shallow tomfool to a sharp and solid young man? I'll tell you what (at least this was the catalyst for part of my evolution experience); it wasn't self respect, it wasn't Jesus being ticked off at me, it wasn't via watching Tim Dunn on Project Runway. It was a vision of a UFO: An Unidentified Female Object. Yep, seeing a gorgeous girl caused me to take on disciplines and practices that heretofore I blew off with a vengeance.

> *After beholding the gorgeous girl of my dreams I became personally disciplined.*

After seeing this vision of beauty, no one had to tell me to comb my hair, or to quit checking for hemorrhoids in public, or to take a bath and clip my braidable nose hairs. After beholding the gorgeous girl of my dreams I became personally disciplined.

Nothing and no one had to badger me to get my act together. Formerly, I couldn't give a flibbertigibbet about cologne, clothes, tucking in my shirt tail, getting good grades—but when I got a vision of the possibility of being with such an amazing female creation of God I ratcheted my life up several notches just so she would notice me. All this new found drive came inwardly and was self-motivating because of what I saw in my mind's eye and the potentiality of it coming to pass.

Having a vision of potentially dating a beautiful girl caused me to quit being the repulsive skinny cave man that I was. It wasn't rules. It wasn't laws. It wasn't getting my butt whipped for bad behavior, but vision. Vision separated me from bad habits and friends and caused me to get focused, by faith, for the female prize.

The positive power that vision brings to life is hardly news.

Solomon said way back yonder that without a vision, people will (depending upon what translation of the Bible you read) cast off restraint, run wild, go naked or perish (Prov. 29:18). In other words, if there isn't anything worth living for, aspiring toward, then people (including your kid) will say "screw it, I'm going to live la vida loca." The apostle Paul, put it this way; if there is no hope then we ought to just pig out and get punch drunk, or as King Jimmy put it, "let's eat and drink because tomorrow, we die." Yes, a "get all you can and can all you get" mentality will naturally fill the void of the vision vapid mind.

> *If life isn't worth living, then your girl will say "screw it!"*

Therefore, dad of a daughter who's going to be tempted by some terrible turd, I strongly advise that you both pray to God she gets His call and until then provide an atmosphere conducive to dream weaving because just hammering her with rules of what not to do ain't going to keep her sane when the hormones hit her brain. No, there has to be an internal switch for something more excellent than temporary gratification that gets flicked inside of her that makes her want to move away from life destroying habits and people and press into greatness.

The Way She Should Go . . .

I know a lot of Christian parents who wonder why their daughters have wandered off the faith reservation when they have raised them with right principles. They've done their best, they weren't perfect, but they did a pretty damn good job trying to set an example and communicate why they live counter to this whacked culture. They gave their girl all the principles and particulars of God and the Gospel and yet, it seems as if it was all for nothing.

Look, (and this is going to be raw) but laws, rules, principles and regulations alone aren't enough to keep your kid from doing crappy things and running with a high voltage dolt. Read St. Paul's letter to the Romans, chapter seven, if you don't believe me.

There has to be something more personal and inspirational other than "thou shall not" to keep your niña away from los wastoids. I believe through Scripture, history and experience your daughter will clue into the divine purpose for why she's landed here on planet earth. I hate to lay this on you, dad, but as the alpha male of your castle, you've got to create an atmosphere of greatness to keep your kid from diving into asinine baseness. Yes, you have to be an inspirational source and provide a rousing environment to help her find her funky bottom line bass note that God almighty wants to drive her life. Here's what I'm talking about . . .

> *"Train up a child in the way he should go and when he is old he will not depart from it."*
> *(Prov. 22:6)*

> *Laws, rules, principles, and regulations alone aren't enough.*

Most parents at their child's baby dedication or baptism are charged by a pastor or priest with the above verse in relation to their newborn infant. Serious parents go to work establishing the principles of God in the hopes that their daughter won't grow up to be Courtney Love. Yes, believing the promise is that if they train them right they won't depart from right living. However, from what I've seen most, Christian kids raised "right" blow off everything they've been taught once they hit puberty.

This presents quite the conundrum to the Christian parent. Has God lied to us? Is this a bunch of holy crap? He supposedly told us through His word to train 'em up in the way they should go, and when they get old they won't turn into a stripper. A lot of us did the best we could only to be sadly disappointed as our kids systematically diss all that we hold dear and know for certain will preserve their dorky know-it-all backside from disaster.

> *Many kids blow off everything they've been taught once they hit puberty.*

So back to the query: Has God lied to us. Is Christopher Hitchens right? Have we been madly duped by a divine masochist? Is this an anachronistic bogus book full of flippin' fairy tales? Or have we failed by not giving them enough 411 or by doing it in the wrong manner? Or...or, have we misinterpreted that verse and thus misapplied the principle, and that's the reason the girl's gone wild?

For the sake of time and context, I blame the latter. Traditionally, Proverbs 22:6 has been interpreted as it is the parents' job to tell their kid what they should do, and doing this will secure them as good kids forever. But it hasn't. Historically, the emphasis has been on what they must do. You know...don't be a hooker, don't chain smoke Camel no-filters, don't drink Jagermeister at a Snoop Dogg bong party, don't lie, don't vote for Hillary...this is what you should do!

> *Has God lied to us. Have we been madly duped by a divine masochist?*

Here's where we've missed it. We've emphasized for centuries the wrong word in that text. The operative word in that verse is not *should* but *they*. That little distinction makes a huge honking difference in child rearing. The difference is that it is the parents' job to help the kid under their care to discern the way they should go and facilitate that bent instead of simply dictating to them what they should do.

Now, certainly we're to teach our kids the differences between right and wrong (duh). The difference from when they're being a racehorse and a jackass. However, Solomon isn't talking about laying down the moral law in this text but rather training a child to be proficient in their purpose. Here, the parent is being called to understand their kid's righteous bents and God gifts and help to facilitate their unique funkiness. Don't believe me? Check it out in the Amplified translation of the Bible . . .

"Train up a child in the way he should go [and in keeping with his individual gift or bent], and when he is old he will not depart from it." (Prov. 22:6)

I believe the key to keeping your daughter away from negative punks is to make possible her positive purpose. Stoking her God-given passions versus endlessly badgering her about not breaking the 10 Commandments will actually cause her to move away from destructive people, places and things.

> *The key to keeping your daughter away from negative punks is to make possible her positive purpose.*

As you train her to pursue her grand passion you begin to see her judge things based upon whether or not they jack with her calling. You'll see her bypass people and things if they are distracting to her desires. Yep, the dreamy dude will lose to the daring dream, the ultimate goal will trump the ubiquitous trolls.

One important thing to remember, dad, when you're training up your girl in the way she should go is that it is her life, her dream, her vision that we're talking about here, not yours.

This is between her and God. This is not about you making her to be something you want her to be but helping her to discover what the Creator wants her to be. Can you dig it?

This can get freaky if you're a fastidious parent. If you and your wife are both doctors and your daughter has a passion for jackhammers, what are you going to do? Scrape her frontal lobe? A lot of parents freak out when their kid has different turn-ons, gifts and abilities and attempt to push them away from what they like and force feed them what fuels their flame.

> *Pay attention to her drives and her likes. Then help her make it happen.*

One glaring example of this was with Winston Churchill. Churchill's parents wanted him to be a lawyer or a doctor, so they sent him to school to prep him for that role. However, Churchill hated it and had no problem letting everyone know it. While doing what his parents thought he should do Churchill's grades tanked, he fell out of favor with his father and so to "punish" him they sent him to military school. Hello! Churchill found his groove. He was a warrior, not a lawyer. Once in the academy Winston excelled...if he would have stayed where his parents put him he'd become a ticked off "good boy" living a life of quiet desperation rather than the one destiny had called him to.

Dad, your job is to righteously and lovingly coach and steward that unique little female gift God has entrusted to you. Pay attention to her drives and her likes and then begin to ask your little señorita bonita . . .

What flicks your switch? If you could do whatever you wanted to do (and it was righteous) what would you do? Ask your daughter these questions:

What do you enjoy doing the most?

What makes you feel like you're in your groove?

What makes you happy?

What really pisses you off?

What do you think God would like you to do?

What talents do you have?

What spiritual gifts has God plopped on you?

What makes you stand out from others?

How do you want to have history write you up?

Are you willing to work your butt off to accomplish these things?

Will you separate from negative people to achieve your purpose?

Do you think this book is the greatest book ever?

What leaders and people are you shadowing to accomplish these goals?

What people both alive and dead inspire you?

Where do you want to be five years from now?

In short, do you wanna be on your way to your dream or an overweight slug sitting in a trailer house watching some crazy talk show host manifest her demons on afternoon TV with your feckless friends?

Set the Stage

> Make your home a healthy spiritual, intellectual and recreational environment that is positive.

One thing my wife and I have determined to do is to provide for our girls an eclectic group of young and old, male and female, black, brown, yellow and white accomplished friends and families who bring a positive visionary chutzpah to the table. This helps us help them get connected to other dreamers in a vision-rich environment.

They're around doctors, lawyers, military personnel, diplomats, martial arts experts, rock stars, authors, pundits, fishing captains, professional hunters, surfers, TV and radio personalities, movie producers, entrepreneurs, artists, student activists, missionaries and ministers from all over the world. We make certain that they are exposed to people that have a vision for something more than just getting by and following the predictable path of the status quo.

We made this happen. We did this on purpose, both for us and for them. We understood the power of being around folks who have something going on in their life and how it rubs off on us and our little chickadees.

Therefore, make your home a healthy spiritual, intellectual and recreational environment that is so positive, powerful, whacky and fun that the alternatives a thug and bad boy offers to your daughter has zero appeal. I'm talking none, nada, nothing, zero, zilch in regard to tempting your kid away from the sweet crib and friends she's been blessed with.

> Don't allow her to turn into a nerve-grating pain in the butt just because she can yodel and juggle oranges.

Not only do I make certain that our home, church, and my work networks are stuffed with sharp, solid and smart people who are pursuing some holy grail, I also make sure my girls have books, videos, movies and music that inspires them to greatness instead of sitting around and griping and moaning. I know most postmodern mediums of entertainment for kids have content that sucks worse than an airplane toilet, but there are many artists and products still out there that will put grist in your girl's meal. It's your job, dad, to make certain your kids have the correct entertainment diet coursing through their skulls. Never underestimate the influence of the songs they hear, the shows they watch and the books they read.

A Balancing Caveat

When I advocate raising your daughter with a sense of vision and purpose, I don't mean turning her into a deluded me-monkey that has the family wrapped around her narcissistic axle. We have seen way too much of this crap in our culture; namely the quasi-talented kid running the family circus.

Look, I know your kid's special, but she's not that special. She's not so extraordinary that she can treat people poorly, especially her family.

She's not so singular that she cannot get off her butt and help around the house.

Dad, you must swear to God here and now that you will not allow your little princess to turn into a nerve-grating pain in the butt just because she can yodel and juggle oranges.

True vision is God-honoring, gracious, loving, just and sacrificial. It is not obsessed with fantasies of fame and power but rather a higher calling of how one can sacrificially help God and man. Make sure daughter gets that memo.

EIGHT

Teach Your Daughter
to Despise Anti-Intellectualism

From the song, *Stupid Girls*, by Pink

"Stupid girl, stupid girls, stupid girls
Maybe if I act like that, that guy will call me back
Porno Paparazzi girl, I don't wanna be a stupid girl."

Have we, as a nation, become completely fascinated with stupid chicks—or what?!? Dad, if you want to have our society's spotlight shine down on your daughter for no real reason other than she's an idiotic, drunken narcissistic chick, well then... this is her window of opportunity! (Remember: the opportunity of a lifetime must be seized within the lifetime of the opportunity. You can get more successful loser principles from my book, *10 Habits of Decidedly Defective People: The Successful Loser's Guide to Life!*)

Yes, if your girl...

1. Is a semi-decent looking ditz with fake, cantaloupe-sized ta-ta's,

2. Is a mediocre singer who can sort of dance at the same time,

3. Is able to quasi-convincingly deliver a line when directed,

4. Doesn't mind stripping once a Diddy song starts spinning,

5. Is cool with having her crotch photographed more often than the Grand Canyon,

6. Is okay with sleeping with various animate and inanimate objects while being filmed,

. . . then you need to get her an agent because she has all the makings of star! I guarantee, dad, that your niña, with the above "qualities," is about to become very rich and famous in this vapid and fetid postmodern milieu.

Americans, it seems, can't get enough of the dumb chum that emits from the splooged brains like those of Lindsay, Britney, Paris and their wannabe ogling ilk. No wonder al-Qaeda calls us the Great Satan.

Y'know, it wouldn't be so bad to see these whacky wenches on our air waves if the media was fair and balanced in showing an equal chunk of accomplished women who have risen to notoriety without having to shine Clinton's apple. But that ain't gonna happen, at least not anytime soon. Maybe after the next terrorist attack on US soil wakes us the hell up, but not for now. As a culture, we have officially traded the applause we used to give to the truly noteworthy and have bestowed it upon the nebulous tramp.

> Human beings, are remarkable for their disinclination to learn from the experience of others.

Indeed, if you get your worldview from E!, Bravo Channel, VH1 and MTV you'd think most girls don't want an education, a righteous vocation, respect from decent people, excellent health, a happy family and the enjoyment of a long and fulfilling life.

With the phenom of Lady Gaga, Britney Spears, Girls Gone Wild and Internet porn, it seems as if today's ladies would rather be known for no panties, making out with their girlfriends at Coyote Ugly, snot-slinging drunkenness, and having their college orgies broadcast on YouTube rather than wisdom and integrity. Some girls are chomping at the bit to step into Anna Nicole's now vacant bra and replace her as the next human chum slick.

You'd figure that after Anna Nicole Smith self destructed, died and went to an early heaven (cough) that loose and loopy lasses everywhere would have learned a lesson. However, as Douglas Adams said, "Human beings, almost unique in having the ability to learn from the experience of others, are remarkable for their apparent disinclination to do so."

Stupidity is still so, so, so...hot!

Anna Nicole Smith Syndrome and Paris Hiltonitus

Girls who wish to wallow and follow in Anna Nicole's footsteps have what I've discovered and defined Anna Nicole Smith Syndrome (or ANSS).

This sickness effects mostly low-income girls from small towns who have, for whatever reason, decided to blow off education, God and true achievement and instead get rich through raunch.

Symptoms your daughter might have ANSS:

Does she have a lifetime subscription to National Enquirer?

Does she take notes while watching Desperate Housewives or the OC?

Does she get drunk in public and yell at unseen people and small animals?

Does she take her top off if someone dares her or if they give her a cold beer or, for that matter, a hot beer?

Does bad press appeal to her?

Does she DVR The Rock of Love?

Does she have a burning desire to jam sacks of silicone into her chest when she's 13?

Has she had two or more unnecessary plastic surgery procedures before she turned 22?

Does she have a proclivity to have sex with the first 89-year-old drooling billionaire she can hold down?

This anti-salubrious sickness is not always fatal but it is always, eventually, viciously debilitating. Unique to this virus is that it is deceptive in its early stages as it makes its carrier seem empowered, invincible, liberated and loved by horny middle-aged men and vapid male masturbatory and marauding teens.

However, as the infected grow older and uglier and the buzz around their antics wears thin, their narcissism spins out of control as they lose public appeal. In addition, their youthful liberties turn to harsh slaveries, and the crowd that laughed with them at the beginning now laughs at them until their brutal end. It is at this point that the girl with ANSS, contracted by a life of bad decisions, begins to get viciously fish slapped by a lifetime of inane choices.

There's also a similar malady called Paris Hiltonitus (PH). This affects mostly privileged girls who squander the insane family benefits afforded to them. The symptoms and diagnosis are very similar to ANSS, except for the sex with the 89-year-old guy stuff.

> Conservatives and Christians are instructed not to judge brainless babes.

The distinction here is that sex with a guy that old, for a spoiled PH girl in her 20s, is "so not hot" or necessary. No, instead one sees these diseased lasses usually copulate with some guy in a boy band or a reality show "star" or a guy who's famous for being famous. Symptomatic to this lot is the compulsion to not only have mechanized sex but to also film their sophomoric sexcapades and float their footage on *heavy.com*.

But Then Again...Who Are We to Judge?

Conservatives, and especially we Christians, have been told that we should not judge such brainless babes but rather help these dregs fulfill their dreams—even if they are not our dreams. We're commanded, in this day of coast-to-coast butt kissing, to remember and obey the 11th Commandment of postmodernism, namely, "thou shalt not judge."

So, instead of offering some legalistic and graceless judgmental blast toward those "ladies" who are following (or wallowing) in Anna Nicole's path, here instead are eight helpful tips to assist you the, father, in helping your daughter to become the next anti-intellectual and immoral train wreck.

Are you ready? You are? Then let's get busy!

1. Make sure you breed within your daughter a "to hell with education" mindset. For all you Anna Nicole Smithers out there, let me help you. All you need, as a maximum, is an 8th grade

edumication. That's all. Barely finishing the 8th grade furnishes one with enough 411 to make demented, irrevocable, life-demolishing decisions. So, just stop, drop and roll right there, girl. Anyway, everyone knows that 9th grade can be real yucky. With all that English blah, blah, blah…and the Algebra, crazy letter, math fraction whatever junk…and that PE stuff and the World History yada yada. Puh-leez. You don't need all that, girlfriend. Hel-lo!

2. Make sure your daughter blows off common sense and gets married when she's 17 to the first 16-year old fry cook she meets. This little brain fart will get her the heck away from the house and all those people who rain on her dream of being the center of the universe.

3. To be an effective Anna Nicole Smither make sure your girl's got an idol to emulate. I recommend choosing a deceased, drug abusing, divorced multiple times, lost soul known only for her looks, her promiscuity and her booze and dope dependency who died at a really young age as her god. Have your daughter put her posters on her wall. Encourage her to act like her hero. Have a plastic surgeon carve up her body to look like that icon. Then, allow your kid to go bonkers doing what she imagines her Yoda would do if she wouldn't have OD'd on Nembutal. In addition, determine that your daughter sells her soul down the river and fully employs her faculties to become recognized as an equal (or a better) ditz to the dead chick she worships. She must have a vision.

4. When earning minimum wage starts slapping your child around, instead of getting an education, retooling and rethinking her multiple idiotic decisions, just encourage her to start showing guys her boobies. She can begin wherever she is. Tell your girl that she can make good money doing this. And we know life is all about money, don't we? For instance, she can do this for cash in the break room at Wal-Mart or next to the deep fryer at Krispy Fried Chicken (watch out for that hot grease, though!). Once she plows through decency and her conscious has decayed enough, I would then go public with her act. Look, her body is what God (if there is a God) gave her, so why

shouldn't she trade off of it? I can't think of any reason not to. A girl's gotta do what a girl's gotta do, right? Y'dam right.

5. When your daughter, the Anna Nicole Smither, begins a life of stripping or some other form of pornography, the probability of becoming self-conscience about not having 36EEE puppies might start to wear on her. If she happens to be mammary challenged, she needs to follow Anna Nicole Smith's lead and jam huge silicone sacks into her chest. On second thought, forget the silicone and have her stuff her chest with 15lb Everlast medicine balls. Kawabunga! That'll get her some Benjamins.

6. To move up the Anna Nicole Smithing ladder, your chica must give a lap dance to some billionaire Methuselah who looks like Gollum after a two-day tequila binge. I'm talkin' about a very, very wealthy and nutty octogenarian. Not only that, but she's got to bump and grind him so well that he coughs up not only his dentures and the Similac snack he had that afternoon, but a wedding ring and half a billion dollars. C'mon girl. Snap that thong, snap that thong, get a diamond ring and bang that gong!

7. Another thing that'll help your girl scoot on down the Anna Nicole Smith road is for her to turn her vagina and all other orifices into a 24-hour convenience store. Yes, when she wants something like a Louis Vuitton purse, a Mercedes, a Tiffany charm bracelet, a breast upgrade, lip injections, Methadone, the principle part in a D-grade lesbian sci-fi flick or a house in the Bahamas...well, tell her the best way for her to get her way is to have sex with whoever has the denari (remember point 6!). That's easier than all that workin', schoolin' and waitin' nonsense, isn't it?

8. If your wannabe Anna Nicole Smither chooses to procreate, just make sure she does not cease her selfish and hellish lifestyle and that her kids get swamped in her wake. First of all, if she wants to have a child, instead of having her kid with one man that she loves, I suggest she have intercourse with several men in ages ranging from 20 to 70, from photographers to princes. Secondly, to make sure her mayhem has a multigenerational effect, drinking and doing drugs while she's pregnant is a good

way to accomplish this end. Thirdly, as her child grows, let him see that she never abandons her destructive habits. Fourthly, if her weirdness doesn't seem to be adversely pummeling her child, then make certain she surrounds herself with creepy, opportunistic lawyers, folks with better drugs, TV producers who'll give her big money for staying wasted and "yes men" who'll never tell your girl that she's a stupid, stupid woman.

Remember to tell your ladies, when they're attempting to court catastrophe and don't know what to do, simply to pause and ask themselves the question, "what would Anna Nicole Smith do?" Then follow suit (keeping the above list handy is helpful, too). Also, you might want to have a WWANSD bracelet made for inspiration.

Look, Anna Nicole didn't live long, but she looked like she was having fun—didn't she? She was on TV a lot, which was pretty cool. Since we have evolved from the fairy tale stage of religious beliefs in all that personal accountability, salvation and damnation stuff, we can rest assured that Anna Nicole has simply passed (as she will also) from one party to the next. Therefore, proceed on, girlfriend, and keep on Anna Nicole Smithing. Keep Anna's anti-intellectual dream alive!

Show Intelligence

Now for those fathers who do not wish their daughters to follow in Anna's path of anti-intellectual self-destruction and would rather have your daughter known and rewarded for her wits rather than her tits, herewith is a sure cure for such an ill.

First off, father, you must have a counterculture blueprint to follow so that your child doesn't end up as blue material for late night comedians. As a Christian, I'm to get my cue for my kid's character from the Word of God and not from this head up its backside culture. Scripture isn't our sole source for role models, but it is a solid stonking font of inspiring dudes and dudettes.

> Daniel was a massive example of propriety amongst a stack of lawless lemmings. and thrived as a godly example in a scat-laden culture.

There are several shining examples of young men and women throughout the scripture that one would do well to emulate. One of my favorites is the prophet Daniel (I even wrote a book about him titled *Ruling in*

Babylon. Check it out!).

Daniel was a prophet who lived 2,600 years ago in a pretty promiscuous place (Babylon) under the authority of a king who would make Bill Clinton look like John the Baptist (Nebuchadnezzar). Daniel, as a teen, was separated from his people, his temple and his godly heritage and thrust under the thumb of a demonic quack and a raunchy culture and yet, he didn't turn into Kevin Federline.

Babylon, though wicked, wasn't unappealing. One of the most decadent kingdoms in history was also more seductive than Kim Kardashian in a black leather bustier. Yes, Babylon had a dizzying array of options and temptations all for the young teen's hormonal delight and Daniel, stripped from his people and props, with (seemingly) no way out of this negative place, and tempted and indoctrinated daily to bend over and blend in, amazingly didn't capitulate to the societal swill but instead became a massive example of propriety amongst a stack of lawless lemmings.

Yes, stunningly Daniel thrived as a godly example in a scat-laden culture. He rose to a place of power and prominence because he wasn't like all the other Babylonian brain dead losers and not only that, the young man effectively turned the King away from idols and unto God. Not too shabby for a teen.

> *Daniel was disciplined, non-conforming, and didn't whine and cry. He cowboyed up in a really bad situation.*

So...how'd he do it? Well, I'm glad you asked. He was disciplined. He didn't go with flow. He didn't whine and cry about how bad things sucked. He cowboyed up and lived a life of excellence which made him a force to be reckoned with, an agent of change. Doesn't that sound tasty?

Of the seven things Daniel disciplined himself to become, intelligence in every branch of wisdom was on the top of his list (Dan. 1:3,4). Shaping up the silly putty between his ears caused him to blow past the dolts of his day. Yep, Daniel realized that if he was going to excel then he was going to have to get smart.

You see, it wasn't enough that Daniel loved God. It wasn't enough that he believed God loved him and had a wonderful plan for his life. It wasn't enough that he had religious T-Shirts and bumper stickers. It wasn't enough that he listened to religious music, gave tacos to homeless people, went to four Bible studies a week and was still a virgin. That was fine...that was cool. But for Daniel to be a leader versus a sheep, for him to separate from the hellish herd and impact and change a secular environment, he had to bring more than sweetness and personal virtue to the table. The boy had to bring brains to the plate or else, in life, he would be more ignored than DJ Qualls at a Beyonce slumber party.

Leaders are Readers

Daniel distinguished himself from the thugs of Babylon and was feared, respected and ten times better than all the Chaldeans because he was smart. It was not because he had the right hair cut, knew the right people, wore Izod polos, had straight teeth and drove a Beemer. It was because he was intelligent and a man of understanding.

Unfortunately, reading among young adults is about as popular as Michelle Obama showing up at David Duke's family reunion wearing a Malcolm X T-Shirt and discussing the outrageous lack of Black Panthers in public office.

Most young folks just don't like to read. Subsequently, they don't lead but rather follow specious fellows of the baser sort. One of the reasons why kids don't read is because, thanks to modern media, they have developed the attention span of a ferret jacked up on Red Bull. If something doesn't scratch their itch, stroke their soft underbelly, arouse them immediately and quickly solve a long-term problem and do it in stereo surround sound...well, then, the heck with it! It's time to move on to the next buzz.

> *Build your daughter a killer library covering a wide variety of topics.*

The young idiots of today often rely too heavily on TV for diversionary info and enjoyment instead of reading. But if we want to change our world, we're going to have to take a tip from the Cable Guy: Kill that baby sitter and then pick up a good book.

I personally loathe the menial level of my past literary intake. Prodigious I was not. Spending twenty-one years skating through school trying to read as little as possible because Pink Floyd told me, "We don't need no education," left me working at a gas station, smoking weed and being one audition away from the lead role in *Dumb and Dumberer: When*

Harry met Lloyd.

Christ had to drag me into His kingdom in order to change my view of education. His pulling me out of the miry clay not only freed me from serious iniquity but also gave me a desire and a reason to extract my head from my backside. Since that salvific experience my wife and I have emphasized (by example) to our daughters the importance of reading widely and deeply if they want to distinguish themselves from the herd and eschew the idiots.

Build a Library

In my book *Ruling in Babylon,* I tell the parent if they desire their young 'uns to become something they're proud of, e.g., kids who don't become pimps, whores or welfare brats, the parent has to do whatever it takes to build for their kids a killer library covering a wide variety of topics. Here are some basic categories to get you started:

The Bible: Get one and—as odd as this sounds—encourage them read it, from stem to stern. It doesn't help them to have it on their nightstand. It's not a lucky charm, even though it is magically delicious. Have them actually read it and make it their book of books.

Study Aids: Purchase a concordance, a lexicon, a standard dictionary, a thesaurus, an exhaustive Scripture reference guide, a Bible dictionary and a Webster's 1828 dictionary. Sure, you'll be out a little cash—but they're going to use them for the rest of their life. Changing the world is a costly venture. So pay the price.

Theology: The other day I heard a girl say, "I don't like theology...I just love Jesus." I replied in my usual first-Corinthians-thirteen manner: "Excuse me, Mrs. Bodine, but what turnip wagon did you fall off of, and which wheel ran you over?"

The fact of the matter is, you can't love God rightly if you don't know Him Biblically. The study of theology is not just a matter of orthodoxy, but one of love. Every Christian is a theologian—either a good one or a bad one.

For God's sake, your sake, the Church's sake and the unbeliever's sake—study the Word. Study in order to make you wise unto salvation, but also to make you effective and powerful in explaining it to others—both sinners and saints, both the learned and the supermodel.

Take your faith seriously!

Biographies: Have your girl read about the lives of great men and great women of God who had powerful ministries, influenced godly political change, fought for human rights, fed the poor and sacrificed everything to reach men for the glory of Christ. Read about their struggles, their failures and their triumphs. Then encourage your daughter to follow those good ole' shampoo instructions: lather, rinse and repeat. Yep, apply their actions, faith and attitudes in the situation to which God's presently called them.

Books on the Martyrs: Here's some unnerving reading: the cost that a few brave hearts paid to advance the Gospel. Reading about the martyrs will give your girl an historical object lesson of people who actually believed the Gospel and lived it out to the point that it cost them their lives. In addition to this, it gives great perspective to our problems, revealing that the great majority of what we are going through is tremendously inconsequential...a mere molehill in the Garden of Eden.

> Reading about the martyrs will jerk any grumbling and lukewarm slack out of her spiritual life.

The martyrs will shake your baby to the core and jerk any grumbling, complaining and lukewarm slack out of her spiritual life.

Philosophy and Philosophers: Most folks who major in philosophy in college usually end up selling bongs at head shops. Philosophy is seen by the average American to be about as useful in "real life" as Emily Post's books are to a Courtney Love concert goer. Nevertheless, this discipline (even if it doesn't seem like an urgent imperative to know and understand) affects not only the way we think, but just as importantly, the way we live.

Philosophy takes a closer look at the ideas behind how we live our lives. What we believe to be true affects our view of ourselves, how we treat other humans and the world in which we live. Though it doesn't seem like there is a lot of thought involved in modern media, most conversations, TV, politics and educational policy—be assured, these all stem from a system of thought. Therefore, we must recognize these thought systems in order to first deconstruct the destructive components in them that lead to the demise of our culture and then recon-

> Philosophy helps your daughter recognize what is being said, where the ideas come from and where they are going to lead.

struct a more excellent way according to God's wisdom.

Studying philosophy is a must, as it helps the young person to recognize what is really being said, where the ideas come from and where they are going to lead.

History: Those who don't learn from the past are doomed to repeat it. If you don't believe me, just ask Snookie.

There is much to be learned by pausing to look backward and then chilling out and thinking about what has transpired up until now. When one studies history, one quickly begins to see the prosperity of nations that honored God and the dissolution of those that turned their backs on Him. Studying our past give us discernment for our present decisions and wisdom in our plans for tomorrow.

The Classics: Because today's youth have the concentration level of a whitetail deer on crystal meth, a working vocabulary below that of Snoop Dogg's Macaw, the passion of JWoww wanting to answer the ultimate questions of life, and a total IQ less than the front row of an American Idol concert—the Classics today stand even more neglected than Rosie O'Donnell's Ab Blaster.

> Classics today stand even more neglected than Rosie O'Donnell's Ab Blaster.

According to Os Guinness, when most people think of a "classic" today, they don't think of a book, but a Coke, or a 1950s roadster, or perhaps an early Beatle's song. Mark Twain defined the problem. He said "a classic is a book that people praise but don't read."

Why is it necessary for young adults to read the classics? Shouldn't only the geeks wearing flood pants read this stuff, while the beauties spend their time loitering at the mall and listening to transvestites on the iPod?

According to Dr. Louise Cowan, we all are to read great books because, "They have been found to enhance and elevate the consciousness of all sorts of people who study them, to lift their readers out of narrowness or provincialism into a wider vision of humanity. Furthermore, they guard the truths of the human heart from faddish half-truths of the day by straightening the mind and imagination and enabling their readers to judge for themselves. In a word, they lead those who will follow into a perception of the fullness and complexity of reality."

Within a society that screams for our daughters to pay attention to the minutiae and the immediate, foregoing contemplation upon the eternal and consequential, if your girl doesn't want to be generational carnage, she must read things that are weighty, timeless, inspiring and instructional.

As C. S. Lewis wrote,

> *"We all, therefore, need the books that will correct the charac-*
> *teristic mistakes of our own period. And that means the old*
> *books...the only palliative is to keep the clean sea breeze of the*
> *centuries blowing through our minds, and this can be done only*
> *by reading old books. It is a good rule, after reading a new book,*
> *never to allow yourself another new one till you have read an*
> *old one in between. If that is too much for you, you should at*
> *least read one old one to every three new ones."*

Pop Culture (literature, music, art, video, movies, TV and poetry): Here's where the majority of Christians bite it in their cultural intake. Shallow as it may sound, not keeping up with modern society can be a real detriment to your usefulness to God and in life. Daniel and the boys lived in a society that caused them to undergo more changes than Joan Rivers' face, breasts and tummy have in the last 20 years, and amazingly with each cultural shift, they stayed on top of the board and rode each wave.

If your daughter is going to be a player in life and change for the better the culture she was birthed into, it will demand her staying on top of what those who influence our society are saying and doing. This means reading the contemporary stuff, watching TV, videos, movies and listening to music. But not just listening mindlessly, but as an analyst dissecting the beliefs and values of these temporary icons, as well as their effects upon their audiences and our nation.

I guarantee pops, that if your girl embraces the above intellectual regimen she will not suffer fools, she will not be easily swayed, and she will be a leader among leaders wherever life may lead her. Yes sir, she won't be Pink's stupid girl, she won't catch ANSS or PH, she'll become a force like Daniel, which means she won't have to show her breasts just to get by.

NINE

Teach Your Daughter How to Party

"Beer is proof that God loves us and wants us to prosper."
—Benjamin Franklin

As you know by now, I'm a Christian. As a believer I have no problem whatsoever with either you or me having a mug of beer, a glass of wine, or a snifter of brandy, enjoying in moderation what the good Lord has blessed us with. No, Dorothy, I'm not a teetotaler. Having said that, I'd never encourage, nor drink around someone who, for whatever reason, has no self-control. It ain't worth it. That would be an abuse of my liberty.

No doubt, some of you legalistic 21st century killjoy Pharisees have problems with a Christian drinking alcohol. How do I know? Well, it is because Christianity, as of late, has been chopped down by the likes of you to these six things, namely:

- Not watching or reading anything with the name Harry Potter on it

- Not going to R-rated movies

- Not smoking cigarettes, a cigar, or a pipe

- Not listening to rock music, rap music or hip hop

- Not watching CNN or MSNBC

- Not drinking alcohol

Yep somehow, the greatest story ever told has been reduced to some goofy self-righteous guy's list of dos and don'ts. The funny thing is that the majority of Christian ministers who are fierce about not drinking are not so vociferous about the ton of food they eat, or the gossip they spread, or the unforgiveness they harbor, or the many hours they spend online viewing porn.

> *Jesus gets perturbed when I have a 12oz bottle of beer, but he's completely cool with you eating chicken by the bucket,*

I was watching Christian TV the other day as this chunky and sweaty minister, who was at least 150 pounds overweight (at least!), lectured his flock and the nation on the demonic evils of enjoying a Bud Light. I'm sitting back thinking, "let me get this right, Jabba...Jesus gets perturbed when I have a 12oz bottle of beer, and he's completely cool with you eating chicken by the bucket, hamburger by the pound and pizza by the foot?" How convenient, Pastor Man Tits. And correct me if I'm wrong, Reverend Cletus Klump, but I believe the glutton and the drunk are both condemned in Scripture. Google it and get back to me.

I'll never forget one time I was at a pastor's conference in Texas with about twenty senior ministers from all over the country. (BTW—I don't like most pastor's conferences. What I've found at such "events" are too many egoists fighting over speaking engagements, bragging about honorariums, gossiping about the other guys, comparing the size of their congregations and talking about what kind of wrist watch they wear. What a pathetic bunch of chicks).

Anyway, for whatever reason I went to the meeting, and because pastors love to eat, we went out to the local feeding trough. After we sat down the waiter comes over to our table to get our drink order. All the guys ordered tea, water or some kind of soft drink and I happened to order a Coors Light. A Coors Light, folks. Not moonshine, Jack Daniel's, Everclear, Mad Dog 20-20 or Cuervo Gold, but a Coors Light. This stuff is barely beer.

> *You could hear all the overweight ministers' sphincters tighten in sync at my beverage selection*

At that moment, when I requested a bottle of the supposed "devil's brew," the table turned dead silent. You could hear all the overweight ministers' sphincters tighten in sync at my beverage selection. It was as if I had ordered a glass of blood drained from the necks of six decapitated puppies in veneration of Satan. I only ordered and drank one beer in front of these supposedly mature Christian men, but they freaked out over the whole "evil" of it.

I won't bore you with the ridiculous details, but I will tell you that the guy who freaked out the most was later exposed for doing weird things with some chick at his church. You'd think numb nuts would have been more concerned about the illegitimate, sinful relationship he was having every week with Rhonda in the church broom closet rather than the righteous and biblical liberty afforded to me in the gospel to drink a beer. Nice totemic view of vice, vicar.

Both the Old and the New Testament are rife with celebration (feasts) wherein alcohol was involved. Alcohol was a part of the God-ordained festivities. And it wasn't for medicinal purposes, or because the water was rancid and they didn't have any Evian, and it wasn't a non-alcoholic grape drink like Welch's or Juicy Juice. It was a buzz-generating drink just like the stuff we drink today. Period. End of discussion. Deal with it.

(If you'd like a couple of great books that cover the topic of Scripture and spirits get: *Drinking with Calvin and Luther: A History of Alcohol in the Church*, by Jim West and *God Gave Wine* by Kenneth Gentry.)

> *Jesus could have turned water into Mountain Dew or a skinny latte, but he didn't. He chose wine.*

Y'know, I hate to bring the Bible into this, but one of the first snapshots we have of Christ in John's gospel is Jesus, at the wedding feast of Cana, turning water into wine. Now, you do know that he could have turned water into anything he wanted to? Why? Well he's God, for God's sake. He could have turned water into soy milk, orange juice, a banana smoothie, a wheat grass shake, Yoo-Hoo, Coca-Cola, Dr. Pepper, Mountain Dew, a No Foam Half-Decaf Skinny Latte, or a Red Bull—but He didn't. He chose wine. Alcoholic wine. And that would be 12 vats of the fruit of the vine. And...and...that was after all the people had already swilled down the initial 12 mondo jugs of the stuff.

Yes, Jesus filled the wine vats back up, but this time with better vino. This really screws with some Christians' minds because: *a.)*

Jesus is actually enjoying himself at a party with alcohol and not fasting and weeping like all the paintings depict poor Jesus doing and, *b.)* when there is a lull in the soirée because the partiers have floated their keg, Christ works a miracle (obviously completely cool with the Father and the Holy Spirit) and keeps the party hopping with fresh and better brew. At that moment He demonstrated His deity not by healing a cripple, not by turning a napkin into a dove, not by making Oprah skinny once and for all, but by turning water into wine.

So, what's my point? My point is this: If the Son of God drank wine and God "gave wine to make the heart merry," and if your girl is going to be offered it, sooner or later, then you'd better get busy teaching her how to get pleasure from it without going Lindsay, if and when, she decides to drink.

I've seen too many families forbid their kids to drink only to have them go ape crazy once they get out from under their parents' watchful eye (i.e., in college). Yes, it's usually the party-repressed church chick that gets the most hammered during spring break because booze has been the forbidden apple all her life.

> *I've seen families forbid their kids to drink only to have them go ape crazy once they get to college.*

If drinking is done properly in front your daughter (in moderation), I believe that she won't be the girl doing 20 shots of tequila down in Cabo on top of the bar at Hagar's place, nor will she be at one end of a 25" hose sucking down Schlitz from a massive funnel.

At our house we have wine or beer served at nearly at every meal (especially breakfast) and at every party. Nobody gets hammered. Nobody strips naked and starts screaming off my balcony at my Russian neighbors. Nobody drives home blitzed out of their skull. Nobody starts trying to stab anyone in the eye socket with a pool cue after they lose a game of Eight Ball. Everybody relaxes, chills and has a good time. No wild crap whatsoever. (And just kiddin' about the breakfast stuff.)

My daughters have seen this from birth, and ladies and gents, I'm glad they have because they have had modeled before them moderation versus madness, and I believe they carry, at an early age, a mature view of enjoying the fruit of the vine.

The Public Party Scene

> Should you really tell dads how to teach their girls to party, especially how to drink?

As I was queuing up to pen this chapter I had a person question me on the wisdom of including this chapter on "*How to Party.*" This church lady said, "Should you really tell dads how to teach their girls to party, especially how to drink? Of all the things you could write about regarding a father and daughter relationship, you pick partying. Well, isn't that special. I wonder who could have inspired you to do that, maybe... um...Satan!"

To which I replied in my typical Christ-like manner: "Who asked you?" Secondly, if I want your opinion, I'll give it to you. Thirdly, partying should be a big part of our lives (not Gary Busey style excess but a simple and regular enjoyment of life). And fourthly, I want my kids to keep their head, have a good time and be safe when out from under my protective and watchful eye. Especially after the 2005 Natalee Holloway murder. I believe that beautiful girl would still be alive if she could have kept her cool while having a good time.

Speaking of Natalie, the 2005 disappearance/murder of Natalie Holloway ticked me off and stunned me on three different levels:

1. The total obfuscation coming from the pencil-neck geek Aruban teens (i.e., the Kalpoe Brothers), from the Frankenstein-like Dutch punk (Johan van der Sloot) and from his lawless lawyer father. As macabre and irreparably dented as the BTK killer was, at least when he was caught, he came clean. Not so with these palm pilots. There must be a special place in hell for rabble like this.

2. The incredibly decrepit Aruban Keystone cops and their banana republic judicial system who handled this case like MC Hammer handled his finances during the 90s and...

3. The fact that this could have been avoided if...if...Natalie wouldn't have gotten snot-slingin' drunk and would have avoided these little murderous horn dogs.

If she was taught how to party, this good-looking blonde girl wouldn't have a.) gotten smashed and b.) left her friends at midnight to go off with the Netherlands' version of Lurch and the local Mango brothers. Now, because of two bad decisions, because of over-riding her common sense and probably everything her parents had told her not to do, her life is history. What a shame. What a loss. And again—what an avoidable tragedy.

The answer is not isolation for your daughter's protection. There really aren't any Mayberry RFDs to move to anymore, as weird guys seem to be everywhere today. Therefore, it is up to dads to teach their girls to become sharper than a bag of wet mice when they party. Yes, even blondes must cease to be "blonde" when they party in public because as we have seen, it could cost them their lives.

> *Even blondes must cease to be "blonde" when they party in public!*

In order to be safe and still have a good time I've compiled a helpful list of pointers— edited, adapted and paraphrased from *www.safeparty.ucdavis.edu/* and their *"Student's Guide to Social Event Planning."* You can also get great 411 from *The Safety Chick, Kathleen Baty*, at *www.safetychick.com* and from *www.familyeducation.com.*

If followed, I guarantee your daughter will stand a better chance of having a good time and avoid Natalie Holloway's heartbreaking fate.

We're Getting Ready for a Party Tonight

Ladies, before you and your BFFs go out and celebrate, do yourself a mondo favor and get a belly full of grub. Eat, girlfriend, eat. Eating high protein foods will slow down the absorption rate of the alcohol so that your Cosmopolitan won't plow your system all at once and you find yourself either dancing on the bar topless or crying hysterically over your ex-boyfriend after having two sips.

Also, figure out how you're getting to the party and how you're getting home in one piece and without Chlamydia. Do not wing it. In addition, make certain your designated driver doesn't blow off their commitment to sobriety and start doing Jello shots 10 minutes into the party. If the DD does proceed to get hammered, call a cab. As the bumper sticker says, "cabs are cheaper than funerals."

Personally, I wouldn't drink more than two drinks while out.

> *All the regrettable crap in your life will usually come after the second and third drink.*

Never drink more than two martinis, trust me, it's ugly! Here's the rule for martinis: One martini, two the most. With three I'm under the table and with four I'm under the host. If you're going to drink, get together with your friends and set a maximum of how many drinks you're going to have and stick to it. All the regrettable crap in your life will usually come after the second and third drink. Also, have your designated driver yell at you in public if you attempt to go over your limit. Give the DD permission to hit you with a meat hook and drag you home if you stubbornly refuse to listen. Sure, it'll leave a massive hole in your shoulder, but you'll thank 'em later.

As you're warming up in the pre-party bullpen make sure you go out with solid friends and not the cheeky transient you just met at Starbuck's. Moreover, while out decide now that you won't wander off with the ominous Goth guy. If you want to help him through life call an exorcist and have him hosed down with holy water and then smack 'em with a crucifix or something. Determine that you're gonna stick with your sane amigos, amiga and not befriend Slingblade. By hanging together and leaving together it will help prevent unwanted hook-ups with some murderous teenaged Dutch douche bag and his Surinamese idiot friends.

Furthermore, before you partake of the bottle have a little quiet time and ask yourself, "self, why am I going to drink?" Think about whether or not you're drinking for the right reasons. Is it to enjoy yourself and chill? If you're drinking be-cause you're mad at the world, or you're trip-ping out over something some chick said to you on Facebook, or you're trying to get over a breakup with the monobrow bartender at Chili's, remember that alcohol is a depressant and will only intensify the funk you're currently fielding. Things will probably go south if you're sour and start sucking down the suds to make the pain go away. Be afraid. If you've got the blues go to church, not to a bar. If you're mad, go punch a wall instead of drinking spiked punch, or call the exorcist you used on that gothic guy. And think about this—you

> *Think about whether or not you're drinking for the right reasons.*

don't have to drink!

Now We're Stepping into the Twilight Zone

All right, my darling, you're now at the party, you've done your homework, you've set your parameters and now you're ensconced by a ton of people who probably haven't, and they're on their way to becoming straight up goofy wasted. Therefore, you got to watch your backside because you have officially entered The Twilight Zone, and the potential to have both a good time and get hurt is out there. Here are six things to remember when you're around both alcohol and idiots:

1. One thing abso-frickin'-lutely for certain I would do is keep an eagle eye on your drink and your surroundings. I wouldn't trust anybody anymore. Thanks to date-rape drugs and the proliferation of horny losers who can't get a girl other than by drugging a victim, I would always hold your drink with your hand covering the top of it. Matter of fact, just take a thermos with you to a party and drink from it. Get one with a skull on it so you'll look cool. If anyone gives you any flack about it, smack 'em with it. You watch, it'll probably catch on with the other partygoers, and everyone will be carting around skull thermoses but you will have been the first.

    Remember, aside from roofies and other drugs, alcohol is still the numero uno date rape drug. A drunken girl is way more likely to be sexually assaulted than a non-drunk girl. If you don't want to up the chances of getting raped, or catching a life-altering fungus on your vajayjay, or waking up in the morning with the sick reality that you just had sex with Bruce, the fry cook at Denny's then stay away from tequila shots.

2. If you or your BFF feel extremely woozy after only one Coor's Light, get help because you probably just got drugged. Two predator drugs being used are roofies and GHB. Both make you feel drunk after about half an hour. Both can cause amnesia and unconsciousness for three to eight hours. Thus, never, never take a drink from a stranger, and if you're having a drink that must be opened make sure the bartender opens the drink in front of you, and who cares if the bartender doesn't like it. Tell Billy behind

the bar that you're profit and he's overhead, and therefore he's at your beck and call.

3. Here's another little ditty: Slow your butt downnnnnnnn. You've got to pace yourself, señorita, and alternate your drinks with some agua purificato. Give your liver a break. Are you really so thirsty that you have to chug your beer? Who the heck in America is that parched that they have to quickly consume their liquor? I could understand someone from the Sahara desert who's been lost without water for the last three weeks slamming down their beverage, but not you, sweetie. Also, you might want to consider that it takes your liver about one hour to deal with each glass of booze, depending on your size, food consumed, and other factors. You must love your liver if you want to live long.

4. How about another tip? Don't muddle up your drinks. Stick with one type of alcohol. Never switch your grains. Alternating different types of alcohol will raise and lower the sugar in your bloodstream which can cause you to spend the evening with your head in the toilet throwing up the chimichanga you ate for lunch a month ago. Commit and stick to your poison.

5. Don't play Quarters or Beer Pong as the randy guys love nothing more than to get a girl to "play" drinking "games" into a drunken stupor.

6. Lastly, if you go into a room and the guy locks the door, kick him in the nuts and leave immediately. Do the same thing if the big girl from the lacrosse team does it also.

Eloquently Wasted?

Here's a little perk to partying with out-of-control jerks, namely trying to raise them from the dead when they pass out from drinking too much. Yep, just like sitting in the exit row in an airplane, you, the smart partier, have got to help morons who can't help themselves should the piece of Samsonite go into a coma from over drinking in your presence. Yeehaw, huh?

First off, forget the old wives tale that Sanka, or a cold shower, or fresh air or doing some jumping jacks will sober up your wasted friend. However, I read somewhere online that if you shave their head and then brand them with a red hot branding iron that those two things will speed up their recovery. Try it . . .

Look, there is no way to sober someone up swiftly. Realize that all that stuff will not work (except for the shaved head and branding iron remedy). The amount of alcohol in the blood is controlled by the metabolic rate of the liver. It will take as many hours to sober up as the number of drinks inhaled. Having said that I'd still do all the above anyway if the drunk person is not near death. Go ahead, have some fun with them. They've ruined your evening so you might as well get out the video camera and then give 'em a cold shower, some black coffee, put them on a spinning bike, and feed them a hamburger on the floor while rolling the camera. If they repent the next day, cool—if not, upload the video to YouTube and David Hasselhoff them.

> You can't sober up someone quickly. The amount of alcohol in the blood is controlled by the metabolic rate of the liver.

FYI: If a person literally passes out in your presence you should check their breathing to make certain it is normal. Also, get them on their side so that should they barf they will not drown in their own vomit. If their breathing is irregular and they are going Heath Ledger on you do not call Mary Kate Olsen, call 911! In addition, if the person is not breathing proceed with mouth-to-mouth resuscitation and call 911.

When the party starts winding down you still must keep your wits about you because the crap is about to get really deep. First thing to do is to stick with your friends. Guys get desperate during last call, and their sexual advances will come fast and furious. Every flattering thing a guy says during a party is pretty much complete BS. All flattering stuff spoken between midnight and 4AM I guarantee is utter horse hockey.

Therefore, since the BS is going to become very thick (you might need a shovel) you should stick with your friends, and for God's sake leave with your friends. Blow off the doe-eyed, new "nice guy" you just met who is "so sweet" to offer you a ride home. He probably has bodies buried in his backyard and human parts pickled in his fridge.

In addition, as you're getting ready to call it a night, I'd start chugging water if you don't want to have a screaming hangover the next day, and I'd call your buddies to make certain they got home and they're cool and haven't climbed up on their roof naked and started shooting their neighbor's cat with a BB gun.

Party Prep Checklist for the Host

If you're contemplating throwing a party here's a simple to do list to help you keep your party safe and not turn into a Hell's Angels biker rally.

> When the party starts winding down, keep your wits and stick with your friends.

1. Think about whom you're going to invite to your party. If you want a great bash don't invite goofy trash. Keep the guys who'll overdose to a minimum. And do not invite the Courtney Love wannabe who'll pee on top of the dinner table to get attention.

2. Also, you'd better decide pretty quickly what kind of party you want to have and stick to the blueprint. Is it going to be a big, open Ted Nugent *Free for All* or do you want a small and quaint rendezvous? Know beforehand what you want because there's a big difference in what is about to happen to your house. Think how many people are realistically going to show up. If it's a wide-open event, which I don't recommend, you'd better brace for the crunch, and I hope you have plenty of cash to replace carpet, furniture and landscaping.

3. How are you going to get the word out about your party? If you want to keep strangers out of your party then don't put out a general advert at Starbuck's or on Facebook, or on the bathroom wall of a swinger's club.

4. If it's going to be loud, really loud, you might get fined, your neighbors might shoot you, and more than likely the cops will show up. That's always fun. Speaking of cops showing up at

your festivities, if they give a dispersal order, you'd better disperse. Do not dispute the order. Obey the cops if they come or it will get nasty. They have guns, nightsticks, guard dogs and tasers, and they will use them. Your best bet is to shut your mouth and leave the area as quickly and safely as possible.

5. Tell your neighbors that you will be throwing a party and let them know the contact information of at least one sober host in case things get out of hand. This will open the door to letting them contact you before the police come and shoot tear gas canisters through your bay window.

6. As a host, you will be taking on specific responsibilities and potential liabilities. You better ask yourself: "What can go wrong, and what can I do to prevent it?" You are responsible for the safety and welfare of all of your guests. This includes those who are uninvited. Some courts have determined that once inside, even the uninvited person becomes your responsibility. And remember this: There are plenty of creepy ambulance chasers just waiting to sue your backside.

7. Make sure your bartender is not a masochist out to slay college students.

8. Get a bad to the bone bouncer and/or a rent-a-cop who determines who and how many people get inside. Plan how people will be getting in and out of your party. Controlling one main entrance makes it easy to regulate how many people come in and whom you want at your get-together.

You might have to bounce somebody if they get rowdy. This is why having a professional bouncer, or a police officer at your party is a good move. Before warning someone with the possibility of being ejected, give them the choice of dialing the heck down. Give people a chance to stop what they are doing. However, do not hesitate to eject a belligerent jackass. When you eject someone, do so quickly, thoroughly and quietly. Make a note of the time and description of the doofus you just tossed out on his head.

9. Have a sober host who can collect car keys and call 911 if the need arises.

10. Keep food around for munchies and for alcohol absorption. Also, keep non-alcoholic drinks and tons of water around for the natives who choose not to swill.

11. Plan how people will be getting home (taxis, DDs, etc). If there will be a lot of people, think about giving a taxi company a heads up about your party. Remember if you're throwing this bash then you are liable for the actions of people who leave your party intoxicated and again, there are plenty of lawyers looking to sue whomever they can leech onto.

12. Think about where you want people to chill in your house. Section off bedrooms so that no party-goer can accidentally throw up in your sock drawer, have sex on your bed, steal your iPod and laptop and then urinate in your shampoo bottle. Section off any area you don't want people in with furniture, a pit bull, or punji sticks and/or barbed wire or some other barrier. Now would be a good time to place down any cardboard or plastic drop cloths.

13. Before you go to bed make sure to clean up all the garbage left outside so your neighbors don't petition the home association to kick you out.

14. And lastly, if everything went well and people stayed cool, then rejoice over the triumph of having a great gathering without any major catastrophes.

There's no reason why your daughter should not be able to party and have a good time. With the above checks and balances and a massive dose of common sense, a good time can still be had by all. It's your job, dad, to school her in the fine art of celebration.

Cheers!

TEN

Teach Your Daughter How to Hunt

". . . we need to conserve that bitter impulse that we have inherited from primitive man. It alone permits us the greatest luxury of all, the ability to enjoy a vacation from the human condition through an authentic, 'immersion in Nature'...and this, in turn, can be achieved only by placing himself in relation to another animal. But there is no animal, pure animal, other than a wild one, and the relationship with him is the hunt."

– Jose Ortega y Gasset –

As you can tell, I love ticking off as many vapid, anti-American and anti-traditional values blowhards as I can. It is one of the chief joys of my life. However, sometimes I need a reprieve from the rancor and the hell razing.

Aside from needing a break from the bellicosity that is my life, I need a break from the place where I live, i.e., Miami. This place is more plastic than Joan River's face, breasts, ear lobes, tummy, or...yecch! I'm sorry. I just made myself vomit. Excuse me for a sec...okay, I'm back.

In addition to the synthetic scene here in South Florida, the metrosexual madness down here is so sassy and solid it leaves a redneck refugee like me shaking like a junkie for a testosterone reality fix away from the weapons-grade foolishness that unfortunately inundates one of the most beautiful spots on the planet.

Also, I get ill thinking about having to go to the mall, again, and having to ford through all the mall rats, with their fake (or real, I don't care) Louis Vuitton purses, Gucci shades, and their angst over, "whether they should get A/X's skinny jeans or Abercrombie's new ones." Yeah, having to share air with these helix-missing morons and being forced to overhear how bad their lives reek as they scream on their cell phones leaves me with an intense desire to get the hell outta Dodge. Y'know what I'm sayin'?

> *I get ill think-ing about the mall rats with their fake Louis Vuitton purses, Gucci shades, and their angst.*

Furthermore (and I know I'm not supposed to say this), I get weary at times of talk radio and TV talk shows, which happens to be a major chunk of my life. Doesn't it get old, occasionally, hearing the left and right go at each other night after night after night after night? Call me a wussy, but since I don't drop acid or smoke ganja anymore I need to escape.

A cruise is out of the question for me. Being on a disease-laced, slow moving diarrhea ship, filled with stretch-pant wearing, buffet-loving, overweight, pink-skinned drunks who are paraded like lemmings from one overpriced port to the next is not my idea of recreating.

Nothing, as far as I'm concerned, does more for me than getting away and going hunting with my family and friends. Putting massive distance between me and the mall, my cell phone and my email and going beyond the pavement in pursuit of the planet's magnificent game animals or birds is b-e-a-u-tiful to me.

> *God didn't create Adam to live in a condo.*

What do I like about it? My cell phone usually doesn't work.

Just getting out in the wild connects me back to my primal spiritual and physical roots. God didn't create Adam to live in a condo. He made a feral crib for his first man to live and whup it up in with Eve. There is something that the undomesticated does to me that no Lysol-disinfected, five star hotel can provide.

Everything slows down. I'm forced to chill out. I'm not going mach 2 with my hair on fire. I'm forced to shut up and quit screaming. I'm forced to breathe, and the air I inhale in the woods is clean and not some germ-laden, stale, fart-loaded, recirculated office oxygen (I office out of my home).

My senses come alive and are taken to a higher level by pursuing my prey. My eyes, ears, nose, feet and hands kick into gear like they don't when I'm sitting like a drooling, giggling, beer-drinking zombie watching *Seinfeld* on my couch.

It makes me get disciplined. To be a successful hunter requires strictness. To shoot a rifle, shotgun, pistol or bow well takes commitment. To successfully stalk a big game animal and make a clean and lethal shot takes additional dedication. To hunt dangerous game animals requires that I be a seriously focused little monkey. To sit quietly for hours takes Tibetan monk-like tenacity. To chase wild boar through a swamp, cougars over miles of desert mountains, and elk where the air is thin means I've gotta work out during the week, or I'm going to be more lost than Carrot Top watching Brit Hume. The above de rigueur explains why I don't see too many crack heads on the hunting fields. My sport demands you have your act together.

Hunting changes lives. I've seen it several times. I have seen bored adults and kids come alive when the hunt commences. I've watched idiots on drugs lay them down for good because they got a greater buzz hunting with good people than they did snorting crank with their butt munch friends in Hialeah. BTW, for the too cool teen or twenty-something who might not think hunting can be as thrilling as drugs, come with me and confront a 350lb PO'ed wild boar, or come to the glades and hunt gators out of an air boat, or take a shot at a grizzly with a bow, or face up to a hippo out of the water with a double rifle. I guarantee ecstasy, 'shrooms, and a crystal has never, can never and will never give you the buzz that these situations will. You'll mess your pants. Give it a try, girlfriend. You'll be sweating like a hooker in church.

> Give hunting a try, girlfriend. You'll be sweating like a hooker in church.

I connect with friends and family on a deeper level. Life's busy in the city. Sometimes, even the "good" relationships we have with friends and family are about as shallow as a creek in Death Valley. The campfire allows for communication that you do not get when the idiot box is on and everyone is running in fifty different directions. If it wasn't for my dad taking me hunting every year when I was a kid, I probably wouldn't really even know him (which might be a plus for him, but would be a huge minus for me). I feed hundreds of poor people with high protein, low fat, yummy flesh that comes from my kills. I guarantee that I and just three of my hunting compadres feed way more hungry people via hunting than your typical group of 1,000 bleeding heart, yarbling, anti-hunters ever have or will.

There are very few loony liberals. Another great blessing regarding hunting is that I seldom, if ever, run into secular, "progressive," pluralistic, relativistic, big government loving, anti-military, God and country-hating leftists.

Yes, when I'm looking for a break I bound into the swamp, brush or woods with gun or bow in tow in pursuit of one of our planet's amazing game animals. Nothing, absolutely nothing, restores my soul like everything that surrounds the sport of hunting with friends and family. As a matter of fact, my 81-year-old dad, five of my closest buddies and I are gearing up for a black bear hunt as I type. Yum yum.

> *Nothing restores my soul like the sport of hunting with friends and family.*

Hunting, if you haven't noticed, is one of my chief joys. I feel sorry for folks who miss out on the healing effects the hunt brings.

Matter of fact, I think these rehab ladies I've been bashing throughout this book would leave their death dealing behaviors behind if they could get a regular dose of the irregular wild. Yes, I believe they'd find their soul, at least what's left of it. King David said in his famous Psalm 23 that God restored his soul and led him in paths of righteousness, not in a bar, or at the mall, or in a city, or chatting on Facebook or MySpace, or by going to another rock concert, but God getting his boy into "green pastures and still waters."

Born to be Wild

Y'know dad, if I hung around all the buttheads in close proximity to Britney Spears and those Anna Nicole was unfortunate enough to schlep with when she was still kicking and Hollywood was my reality, I, too, would probably:

1. Shave my head.

2. Be wasted during awards shows.

3. Stay completely blitzed out of my brain on dope.

4. Tattoo every square inch of my noggin.

5. Pierce not just my ears and me privies, but the front part of my brain.

6. Pummel parked cars with umbrellas.

7. Walk around town with a pink wig and no panties (I know, it's a scary picture, eh?).

I know I have a black belt in being a loveless jerk; however, I can empathize with their extreme behavior and their indulgence into mind-altering drugs. If I were forced into their situation and had to listen to Bobby Trendy, Howard K. Stern, KFed and Paris' stuff 24/7, I would take bong hits morning, noon and night, mainline Ketel One and drink methadone like it was Yoo Hoo. If not, I'm afraid that I'd be up on murder charges, as I lean more toward being homicidal than suicidal.

Thankfully, drugs, an early grave and murder are not the only option for Brit (or any other girl caught in similar circumstances). One thing you young ladies could do is take responsibility and climb out of that toilet you've gotten yourself into, and muy pronto. That's right, leave your "friends" now. All of them. Including your family, if they have aided and abetted your asininity. Do it. Wherever you are...go! Just take off running in the opposite direction, even if that means into heavy traffic on the 405. Dodging multiple high-speed vehicles filled with scurrying illegal aliens is safer than hanging with the warped monkeys you're around now.

> *That's right, leave your "friends" now. Just take off running in the opposite direction.*

Most folks would say you Britney-types need to go to rehab. I'm all about going to rehab. I'm in rehab right now. I'm trying to get delivered from my acerbic Left loathing, my metrosexual nausea, my America loving, my gun collecting, my God worshipping and my testosterone addictions that the secular progressives say are "wrong."

It's not going very well. I keep on falling off the wagon. Or is it falling on the wagon? Whatever it is, I'm not getting "better." Anyway, this is not about my angst and me. My advice for you, Brit (and those mired in similar Shiite), is not to check-in to rehab with Amy Winehouse, but dive into hunting. Yep, if they got a consistent dosage of the great outdoors, I believe it would by fiat separate them from the shallow whores.

This is easy math, dad, stick with me...

Check it out: Hollywood hates guns, hunting and eating meat, and they spit out the daftest characters on the planet. Therefore, if you don't want your girl to be a Tinseltown divorced multiple times, plastic surgery addicted, booze and dope dependant STD machine, you've got to help her do the opposite of what Hollywood does; i.e., get into guns, hunting and eating meat. It's logical. My grad school profs would be proud of that deduction...I think.

I've noticed in my wonderful world of guns and hunting that we don't have too many drug and alcohol addled freak boys and girls. Sure, there are one or two helix misers in our humongous community, but we pale in comparison to Hollywood's glut of Darwinian throwbacks. It seems as if the bang of the gun, the flight of the arrow, the consumption of freshly killed flesh and the thrill of the hunt are effective in keeping one's feet tethered to the planet.

> Instead of checking into rehab, dive into hunting!

I believe that just as you emasculate a man when you remove him from the wild, you slay a woman when she doesn't get a regular dose of the primal scream of nature—in particular, the hunt. Hunting is an escape and a sensual exchange that getting new hip implants, maxing out a Master Card, and having a porn video made of you and your boyfriend's ham-fisted "love making" attempts could never outdo.

Hey, nutty college chick, you wanna be a "Girl Gone Wild?" Well, good. Women, like men, are born to be wild. Having an undomesticated feral facet to your life is right, and I believe that when you girls do not get a regular release of this rebel yell/huntress/outdoor otherness, you're going to seek out some artificial, and oft times damaging, sensory satisfaction.

Padre, if your bambina likes thrills and chills, I'm talkin' wacky, hair standing up on end, slap your momma, OMG stuff that will blow away anything chemicals or herbs can provide, try this (I know what I'm about to advocate is expensive, but it is cheaper than rehab, an unwanted child, a dumb ass son-in-law, bail money, insane lawyer fees, and it is way cheaper than personal and painful family heart ache):

> *Having an un-domesticated feral facet to your life is right and good.*

1. Take your daughter on a grizzly bear hunt with a recurve bow. If she likes "living on the edge" then get her a primitive weapon and crawl up to a 700lb furry ball of teeth and claws. She'll mess her pants! This will surpass any synthetic buzz she's either toying with or hooked on.

2. Go to Africa and stare down a cape buffalo, an elephant or a rogue bull hippo (out of the water) armed only with an old British double rifle. It's a kill or be killed exchange that's a tad more interesting than another night of tequila shots at Tu Tu Tango.

3. Bound through an alligator and water moccasin infested swamp chasing a perturbed wild boar. I've seen many girls and guys grow a pair and get born again on the spot once the boar they're pursuing ceases to run and confronts the hunter.

4. Run over the Desert Mountains of Arizona following dogs that are hot on the trail of a mountain lion. If you're lucky you might not only get a cougar at close range but you also might get to help the Border Patrol snag a few "undocumented workers." It could be a two-fer. Fo' shizzle it won't be boring.

5. Try, just try, to sneak up on a mature whitetail buck or a giant kudu bull. I bet she can't get within 100 yards before they show you their backside and then leave you in the dust.

6. Fight with a 500-lb bull shark, a 150-lb tarpon, a 7-ft sailfish or a 40lb mahi-mahi. After a day of big game fishing she will be so tired and exhilarated that she won't give a flip about the minu-

tiae her superficial buddies are wrapped up in.

The above is true also for the young women who don't strip, do sex tapes, aren't drug dependant or dating back-up dancers for boy bands. You, too, can be imbalanced and a candidate for a meltdown (though probably less sensational than Brit's) if you don't get out of your regular world of bland and get dirty in the hunt.

> God's first boy and girl were directly connected to the Spirit of the Wild.

It seems like more and more women are catching on to the buzz that is hunting. Thanks to Safari Club International and their Sables sub-division, the Becoming an Outdoors-Woman organization and Fiona Capstick's amazing book, *The Diana Files: The Huntress – Traveler Through History*, the ladies are leaving that which is plastic and entering into that which truly satisfies, i.e., the hunt. I almost forgot to mention this, but major labels are coming out with safari clothes for girls so that you can look svelte in the veld. Praise the Lord and pass the ammunition!

Many women are following their men into the countryside. They, too, want to see sunsets and sunrises, breathe fresh air, see stars, get scared, enjoy a campfire, pursue game, feel the rush, eat the flesh, chew leather and truly get wild—but without the nonsense.

And God Said, "It is good."

I hate to bring the Bible into this, but please note, dad, that the cradle God created not only for Adam but for Eve was rough country—a thorny, critter-laden and butt-kicking badland. God wanted His prototypes brought up in undomesticated surroundings. The feral fashioned something in God's first couple that X-box, the mall and cell phones just couldn't provide to the charges under His tutelage.

Yeah, God's first boy and girl were directly connected to the Spirit of the Wild. Adam and Eve lived in primitive partnership with untamed beasts, birds, big lizards and monster sharks. This is the way it was. And God said, "It is good!" Imagine that: good being equated to having no anti-bacterial gel, no bike helmets, no Trans Fatty acids, no poodles, Fendi, America's Next Supermodel, no iPhones, no concrete and no Gossip Girls. I know this doesn't sound like "paradise" for postmodern pantywaists who are immoral, lazy, stupid and fat, but it was God's—and His primitive couple's—idea of "Yippee Land."

So what do we learn from this preliminary little Bible nugget, children? The lesson is clear: If you want your girl (in this case) to step away from the pusillanimous and lugubrious pomo pack, then you might want to get her outdoors, beyond the pavement, and let the created order carve its mark into your daughter.

I make certain that my two alpha teen-aged females, along with my wife and I, get a regular dose of the irregular wild. Our lives consist of large quantities of surfing in shark-infested waters, biking in the backwoods, workouts on the beach, hunting in the sweltering swamps of the everglades for wild boar, fishing the brimming waters of South Florida, sheep hunting in America's beautiful mountains and treks into the African bush.

> We need it for our souls, our sanity and our spirits in this increasingly plastic place.

Why do we make the financial commitment and time-laden efforts to get away from the Miami metropolis? Well, call us weak, but we need it for our souls, our sanity and our spirits in this increasingly plastic place. The spiritual and ethical moorings that nature affords us cannot be found in the tame and lame wastelands of civilization.

So, take the time—no, make the time, father of the peculiar X chromosomes—to venture out with your girl...away from the city, away from the tidy and predictable...and watch what happens to your baby as she separates from the prissy and is forced to interface with the primal. It is magical.

ELEVEN

Teach Your Daughter How to Avoid the Date from Hell

B eing semi-"out there" in the public eye via my *TownHall. com* column, 'net presence, ministry, a little TV and my radio show, I get to hear from a lot of people. One thing I hear constantly from single girls is their dating and marital horror stories. I hear comments like, "Guys are jackasses, jerks, scum, sleaze bags, dufuses, low lifes, lazy, abusive, etc. . . ."

I'll grant that some of my male brethren can be brutish, but...uh...at the end of the day...unless you're a pre-teen girl who's part of a Warren Jeffs-like FLDS cult, nobody forced you to date or marry said jackass. Ultimately, it's your fault if you find yourself in cahoots with a creep. Somewhere along the line you blew off wisdom, counsel and common sense. I know that's tight, but it's right.

Father, if your girl has blown it relationally, don't despair. There's always hope; however, you've got to help them to wise up. As one of my friends says, "If a donkey kicks you once, it's his fault. If he kicks you twice, it's yours."

So, hermano, how does your girl avoid dating or marrying some festering bag of ripe compost like Kevin Federline and his helix-missing ilk? I know Britney Spears isn't the finest wine in the rack; however, even with her low levels of discernment and her Turkish walnut-like density, I believe Brit (as well as those below and above her in brilliance) can, with a little guidance, steer relationally clear from any urge to m1with some future K-Fedian bad date.

So...how can your girl circumvent the date from hell? Its pretty simple, dad. Teach her the following principles, and (with much prayer and sweat) she'll land a quality catch. Blow them off, and she'll attract some Darwinian holdover who'll drain her emotionally, spiritually, physically and financially more than a hemi-powered robotic milker sucks the leche out of a cow.

Here we go dad, give your girl the following words of wisdom...

Before You "Get" a Boyfriend

Girlfriend, are you ready to leave in the dust some dude who's not worthy of sharing the air you breathe—much less your time and attention? You are? Well, giddy up. Here's the master list that will increase your chances of attracting a prince Charming versus a piece of Charmin.

Before you "get" a boyfriend...

1. Get Focused.

2. Use Your Head Freak Girl.

3. Repeat After Me: "Opposites Attract" is BS.

4. Just Say No To Being a Pirate Hooker.

5. Know When To Tell Him to Back Off.

6. Don't Move into His Crap Apartment.

Number One: Get Focused.

A lot of ladies date disasters simply because they don't have squat going on in their own lives and think that the missing link is regularly French kissing the over-moussed bartender at Chili's. One way to make certain you do not get wrapped around the axle of the date from hell is to make sure you're kicking butt in life first—before you try to partner with anyone else.

Before you wade into the dating swamp, make sure you have something going on. Dissuade yourself right now from the debilitating notion that you need a man to be complete. Granted, great guys do add to the mix. That said, it's incumbent that you first have "a life" for a good man to add to.

> *Before you wade into the dating swamp, make sure you're kicking butt in life.*

A relationship with Rico Suave is subservient to the priority that you are focused. Yeah, you need a vision more than you need a tripod. You need something great to live and die for first. You need to hear from God before you fuse to a fellow. If not, you'll be a gullible Etch-A-Sketch for some scribbling monkey.

Look ladies, if you enter into a relationship rudderless, like a needy parasite, you will become the slave of whatever host you hitched yourself to. You'll find yourself doing things...changing things...believing things...compromising things...and getting involved in crap you wouldn't even think of doing just because you neeeeeeeeeeed him.

Girls get freaky when they don't have much going on in life. They try to over please, which is cool for two to three weeks for most guys, but then it gets a little nerve-gratingly old. Yes, the desire to please motivated from need can get whacked. It goes something like this: Girl - "Do you like my hair?" The guy pauses because he's watching a Bud Lite commercial. The co-dependant girl takes his pause as disapproval and spouts, "What—you don't like my hair? Is it my bangs? It's my bangs, isn't it? 'Cause I'll cut 'em. If you want me to, I'll cut my bangs. I swear to God, I'll cut 'em. Don't leave me! Arggh!"

Honeys, please, please, don't queue up to any person needing them to make you whole. Holy cow, señorita. Looking to most guys nowadays for fulfillment, as one comedian said, is like looking to Carrot Top for psychoanalysis. You've got to go to the desert. Get focused.

You should have (again!) so much going on that if your guy dumps you like a chunk of concrete or if some dude doesn't like you it shouldn't cause a major hiccup in your life. Why? Well, you have a nation to save, a dragon to slay, a mountain to conquer, a mission to attend to and it's that man's loss, not yours.

> *Looking to a man for fulfillment is like looking to Carrot Top for psychoanalysis.*

Listen, if a guy leaves you, or is not attracted to you, that shouldn't derail your existence. That shouldn't throw you into a neurotic never-ending introspective trip that leaves you depressed, jonesing on Bridget Jones, developing raccoon eyes from lack of sleep, or singing "I cant live if living is without you" while you gorge yourself on aerosol whipped cream.

Number Two: Use Your Head Freak Girl.

When someone "feels" they're in love, the first thing to go is all cognizant thought. Yeah, here's where the hormones forcefully kick logic's butt to the curb and begin to drive the girl's life like a drunk (or sober, for that matter) Gary Busey.

When the blood drains from the head to the crotch, men call this enjoyable but often-disastrous phenomenon thinking with their "little head." Though minus the particular member men are guilty of being partial to, girls can also make massive mistakes when their heads switch off and their "hearts" switch on.

> The key to keeping your pretty feet tethered to the planet while dating is to USE YOUR HEAD!

Ladies, the key to keeping your pretty feet tethered to the planet when you roam out into the dating Serengeti is...(drum roll, please)... to think! God gave you a head, so use it. Get a grip. Try to stay sane, girlfriend, so that romance doesn't eclipse common sense.

If you find that you're having problems using your noggin, do these: first, keep your hands off each other 'til your brain catches up with your body. Second, don't blow off family and friends, because they can help you see through the veil of crap that most bad guys hide behind.

Number Three: Repeat After Me: "Opposites Attract" is BS.

Paula Abdul said, "It ain't fiction it's a natural fact, we come together cuz opposites attract." And who are we to question the multiple divorced and serial bad dater, Paula Abduh? Girls, forget Miss Abdul's advice. Sure, opposites attract, but the real question is...will they stay intact when the poop hits the fan? And the answer is, highly unlikely.

Y'know, finding someone like-minded doesn't sound as sexy as dating the brooding, in and out of jail, melancholic, mysterious, exotic wannabe rebel flute player for a Beatle's cover band who needs your breast to lie on in order for him to make sense out of life. Yes, ladies,

> Men will do any-
> thing to get in-
> side your pants.

if you'd like to have a successful relationship with longevity, you've got to blow off the Sugar Daddy, the Tommy Lee or the Olivier Martinez idol you're worshipping and realize that compatibility, not fantasy, is the key to the kingdom.

Number Four: Just Say No To Being a Pirate Hooker.

Not letting the dillweed you just met hump your leg anytime soon is usually a sure-fire way to cudgel off the date from hell. This is no secret: The gibbering monkey that's inside a guy's pants wants inside of your pants, and he'll do anything to get it there, muy pronto. Yes, Pollyanna, men will lie, swear, pretend, go to church, walk backwards, watch Marie Antoinette or Nell, listen to Mariah Carey or Celine Dion, etc., just to unleash the beast.

However, ladies (if you haven't learned this yet, you will) once you let them in they are officially on their way out, and all you're left with is the icky thought that you actually had sex with the guy who drops fries at McDonald's. That's a horrible notion. Plus, there's about a 25% chance that you now have the gift that keeps on giving, an STD. Yippee!

Look ladies, reality is that sex with most guys is as about as eventful as a Cinco de Mayo Fest in Dar es Salaam. Don't believe me? Then ask some of your violated girlfriends after they've had a couple of beers. They'll confirm it. Being virtuous and guarding your garden 'til you get a worthy dude to put a ring on your finger saves you from the

> A guy who
> waits for mar-
> riage is either
> gay or he really,
> really respects
> you.

BS of possibly getting saddled with an STD, or becoming pregnant, or having your soul shattered like an ostrich egg shipped FedEx overnight when the guy finally dumps you for your roommate.

Save it 'til you get married, girls, because a guy who'll wait that long is either gay or he really, really respects you. Hopefully, it's the latter.

Number Five. Know When To Tell Him to Back Off.

Another great way to avoid dating some yard ape is to erect massive boundaries around your life. Have who you are and what you'll tolerate so solidly defined that all goofy guys can read it and weep.

You've got to stay guarded, girls. Let the guys call you stubborn, selfish, holier-than-thou, unfeeling, unyielding, unbeholden and unloving when you stay in your values corner. At least there won't be some porn video of you and him floating around on the internet for your grandparents to have emailed to them via YouTube, eh? With 60-foot tall razor wire prison fencing metaphysically placed around you, you will assure that all suitors will respect you, and you will never be controlled or manipulated by some crotch rocket (which is a big plus).

Number Six: Don't Move into His Crap Apartment.

Don't move into a guy's house. This equals loss of authority. This is a stupid move. Why does this act equal dumb squared? Well, you give a dude all the perks of being married without any commitment. And that's what the date from hell loves: zero commitment. By having as an absolute standard that you will not move in with a guy until you're wed, you will weed out all wankers. The truly great guy will respect you more for your self-control, which, by the way, is a must for any healthy marriage.

TWELVE

The Ten Commandments for My Daughter's Potential Boyfriends

God, in His providence, has seen fit to bestow upon my wife and me two beautiful girls that we must steward into greatness. It has been a blast watching my daughters develop into righteous and rowdy, gorgeous girls. The thing that sucks with their metamorphosis into womanhood is the guys who've begun to buzz around our happy nest interested in my ladies.

As much as I don't like the idea of their dating, I have got to suck it up and accept it (bartender, I'll have a shot of whiskey). All you dads who are worth your salt and give a crap about your kid...you know how hard it is to let your girls go. (I'll take another shot, please.)

Even though I'm slowly coming to grips with my kids growing up, I'm not throwing out my brain and becoming a hip and groovy dad who curls up in the corner in the fetal position without an opinion regarding their dating life.

Not only do I have an opinion regarding wannabe suitors, I have ten commandments for potential boyfriends. Yes, seeing that I'm still the Alpha dog of the Giles castle, that I still pay the bills, buy the SUVs, pay for college and secure their condos, then by God, I'm still makin' the rules. I am Doug Almighty, got that Rico Suave? What I'm about to reveal unto you is an attitude-laden afflatus, so...be afraid. Herewith are my 10 commandments for my daughter's potential boyfriends. Read them and weep:

1. Thou shall understand that your presence doesn't make me happy. Young squire, don't expect me to be giggly when I meet you.

As a matter of fact, you're ruining my life right now. Therefore, don't try to be cute with me. That stuff may work on my daughter or my wife, but it does not work with me.

Actually, you should expect nothing from me in the way of the warm and fuzzies. You've got to earn that. I don't care who you are or who your momma is. Your presence represents a transition that I'm not really ready for, so just stay the heck back and be real cool. And know this: I've got a PI doing a background check on you right now.

2. Thou had better have a life. My wife and I have worked our tails off providing a good life for our girls; therefore, you better have one, Spanky. Let me spell it out for you just in case you don't get it. You must have something positive going on in that thing you call a life.

   Additionally, you must be pursuing said noble goal at Mach 2 with your hair on fire. If you're a slacking, blame-shifting, visionless slug with genital warts who's waiting for someone to carry you into greatness and who lives by the dictates of his ding dong, then you need to find a girl who doesn't have a father like me.

3. Thou shall not touch my daughter, or I'll tear your hands off and you'll have to "whip the bishop" with a stub. Not only am I not cool with your being around me, I'm sure as heck not down with you touching my daughter. Therefore, when you're in my space (and in my absence) you'd better treat my daughters with the utmost respect.

   Do not under any circumstance hang all over my daughter, fondle my daughter or soul kiss my kid until you have a wedding ring on her finger, a joint checking account and MMA at Wachovia—or I will shove your Justin Timberlake backside off my 3rd floor balcony first chance I get, capisce?

4. Thou shall look me in the eye, shake my hand like a man and turn off your damn cell phone. I don't care how Snoop Dog acts

and what you've seen on MTV or in the movies. If you come into my house mumbling, with your shades on and texting the entire time you're around me, you're probably going to be spending the next couple of days in ICU.

I want eye contact. I want you to see my soul, son. I want to look you in the eye when I communicate things regarding my girls and their lives. So, take the shades off, Hollywood. In addition, if and when I extend my hand, grab it like you mean it. Where I come from, a limp hand shake = limp life, Twinkle Toes. Also, when you're at my casa, your phone goes on vibrate. I'm sure you'll like that.

5. Thou shall understand that you are a boy talking to a man. Here's some 411 to meditate upon before you address me. I am at least twice your age. I used to be a drug user/dealer until God zapped me. I've been in many fights. I've shot at felons. I faced down too many to count charging wild boar. I've spent years in Tae Kwon Do. I've traveled the planet. You, on the other hand, use Proactiv and drive a Ford Focus; therefore, you will call me "Mr. Giles" and my wife "Mrs. Giles" until we tell you any different.

Also, don't gush around me nor attempt to read me an entry from your journal. I'm not Oprah or one of your metrosexual buddies that you can share all of your inner fears and deepest needs with. I am a Neanderthal.

6. Thou shall know that our family is old school. Do not even think about approaching me with liberal, hippy, agnostic, atheistic, anti-American or tree-humping bull crap. I was raised by country-loving, God-fearing, hard-working, meat-eating, good ole' Texan parents, and I have zero tolerance for what your long-toothed, rather mannish lesbian sociology teacher at Columbia U programmed you with—you dig?

7. Thou shall know that I like cool and expensive gifts, and you shall provide unto me this bounty, if you're smart. One great way to earn my favor is to buy it. Yes, you'd be shrewd to ap-

proach me like the three wise men did baby Jesus, namely with gold, frankincense and myrrh.

For example, I like high-quality cigars (nothing below a 90), Johnnie Walker Blue Label, Chimay Grand Reserve, books on hunting Africa and old British double rifles. I also like original art work, R&B and classic rock compilations, collecting skulls, hunting and big game fishing trips, antique Christian and Classic books, custom choppers and early twentieth century African safari memorabilia.

Who knows...I might, might, ask you to join me for a nice cigar session with me and the boys if thou comest bearing such offerings.

8. Thou shall understand that if you're dumb enough to tell me a dirty joke, I'm comfortable enough with kicking your butt. I'm not one of your thug buddies you can go down the gutter with. I want maturity when you are around my family.

9. Thou shall keep your word. If you say you're going to do something, then I expect you to do it. You see, I'm looking for stability/reliability for my ladies, and keeping your word in the smallest matters tells me that you're ahead of the pack and at least a consideration, in my mind, for our support.

10. Thou shall do these three things:
   1) Look good. Do not come into my house with earrings, a grill, or oversized pants with your butt cleavage hanging out.
   2) Read. If I have to talk to you, you had better know as much about as many things as possible.
   3) Serve. I'm looking for a sacrificial dude who doesn't mind getting his hands dirty in helping around the house, in our community, in our nation and with our wonderful world. If you, young man, obey all the words written here, then and only then will you have a chance with my babies. Now, go get me a beer!

THIRTEEN
Application for Permission
to Date my Daughter

Note: This application will be incomplete and rejected unless accompanied by a complete financial statement, job history, lineage, and current medical report from your doctor.

Name_____

Date of Birth_____

Height_____ Weight_____

IQ_____ GPA_____

Social Security #_____

Drivers License #_____

Boy Scout Rank and Badges

_____

Home Address:_____

City/State_____ Zip _____

Do you have parents?......___Yes ___No

Is one male and the other female? ___Yes ___No

If No, explain:

_____

_____

Number of years they have been married

_____

If less than your age, explain

_____

_____

Accessories Section:

A. Do you own or have access to a van? ___Yes ___No

B. A truck with oversized tires? ___Yes ___No

C. A waterbed? ___Yes ___No

D. A pickup with a mattress in the back? ___Yes ___No

E. A tattoo? ___Yes ___No

F. Do you have an earring, nose ring, ___Yes ___No

   pierced tongue, pierced cheek or a belly button ring?

(If you answered "yes" to any of the above, discontinue application and leave premises immediately. I suggest running.)

Essay Section:

In 50 words or less, what does "Late" mean to you?

_____

_____

In 50 words or less, what does "Don't touch my daughter" mean to you?

_____

_____

In 50 words or less, what does "Abstinence" mean to you?

_____

_____

References Section:

Church you attend: _____

How often you attend: _____

When would be the best time to interview your:

...Father? _____

...Mother? _____

...Pastor? _____

Short Answer Section:

Answer by filling in the blank. Please answer freely; all answers are confidential.

A: If I were shot, the last place I would want to be shot would be:

_____

B: If I were beaten, the last bone I would want broken is my:

_____

C: A woman's place is in the:

D: The one thing I hope this application does not ask me about is:

E. What do you want to do if you grow up?

F. When I meet a girl, the thing I always notice about her first is:

G. What is the current going rate of a hotel room? _____
I swear that all information supplied above is true and correct to the best of my knowledge under penalty of death, dismemberment, Native American ant torture, crucifixion, electrocution, Chinese water torture, red hot pokers, and Hillary Clinton kiss torture.

Applicant's Signature (that means sign your name, moron!)

Mother's Signature . . . . . .   Father's Signature

Pastor/Priest/Rabbi
State Representative/Congressman

Thank you for your interest, and it had better be genuine and non-sexual. Please allow four to six years for processing.
You will be contacted in writing if you are approved. Please do not try to call or write (since you probably can't, and it would cause you injury). If your application is rejected, you will be notified by two gentleman wearing white ties carrying violin cases. (you might watch your back).
To prepare yourself, start studying the ten commandments for my daughter's potential boyfriend.

Author unknown. One person says that this "was written by John Sherbondy of Council Bluffs, Iowa. It appeared in his wife's column in the Nonpareil Newspaper called Kippies Corner." (abt. 1993). I've tried to contact Mr. Sherbondy to confirm but haven't succeeded yet.

Raising Righteous and Rowdy Girls

FOURTEEN

About My Dad:
From the Author's Daughters

A dad who loves his daughter will do all he can to protect and provide for her. Fathers are a symbol of stability in a girl's life and they need to assume that role. Ever since I was little, my dad spent as much time with my sister and I as he could. He would take us on bike rides around the neighborhood before dinner and then read stories to us before we went to bed. We talked about God, our country, family, friends, and our dogs. He always answered us when we asked questions and was there to help us understand the world.

As I developed a relationship with God and began to grow physically, mentally, and spiritually, the more things I was exposed to that I had questions about. Through all those things my dad was always there to guide me. It seems like every stage in my life has had a purpose, and I had someone strong to see me through each one.

Back in the summer of 2001, my dad told me that I would be starting Brazilian Jiu-Jitsu classes. I was not crazy about the idea and even resisted going for a short time. My parents picked up on my attitude and decided that it had to go. They explained to me that if nothing else, they have given me life, and with Jiu-Jitsu they were giving me the ability to protect that life. My dad said that if I wanted to grow and live a confident, independent life, I would need the tools to make it happen. A confident and independent life sounded good to me; I'm positive that is the desire of every girl.

So, I dove into Jiu-Jitsu, studying and applying the techniques whenever I had the chance. After 9 ½ years of consistent self-defense and grappling training, I would say I am pretty confident that I could protect myself in a sticky situation.

With Jiu-Jitsu, my dad gave me a way to protect myself physically. But he also raised my sister and me in a way that protects our lives beyond the physical realm. School was always important, and we were always encouraged to do well. However, our education was never the sole responsibility of the schools. Talks at the dinner table, shark fishing trips, bike rides, and games of football on the beach were just a few things that I would do with my dad. This time spent together was not only fun, but I walked away with life lessons that I will never forget.

One thing that I cherish the most is when my parents would have their friends over for dinner parties. Toward the end of the night, when all the adults sat down to have their "grown up talks," my sister and I were always welcomed to stay up and sit with them. As a kid it made me feel like I wasn't just a sideshow for my parents and that I was an actual part of their lives.

I think that is where the disconnect between fathers and daughters often occurs in our society. Little girls always look up to their daddies. If dad is not there to take care of them and show them how to truly live, appreciate, and embrace life, then that is when bonds are broken and they seek attention elsewhere.

I respect my dad for raising me the way he has. My young life has met with success and good times more often than not, and I look forward to a fuller life that honors what my parents have done for me. If it weren't for my dad's active role in my life, chances are I wouldn't be the confident, independent, Christian surfer girl who knows how to stand up for what she believes in and isn't threatened by scary situations.

Hannah Giles

Hannah Giles is the young journalist who conceived and executed the 2009 ACORN scandal with James O'Keefe. She played the role of the Prostitute.

Since the September 10, 2009 release of the first video, the Census Bureau declared it was severing all ties with ACORN.

The Senate voted 83-7 in favor of de-funding the controversial group. The House voted 345-75 to cut all funds to ACORN, and more than 20 states have demanded either a full investigation of ACORN or that they lose their funding. The IRS cut their connections to the group, and just recently ACORN has declared bankruptcy and announced it will undergo an official name-change.

Hannah is the eldest daughter of Pastor Doug Giles of Miami, FL. She is an avid surfer and Valente Jiu-Jitsu practitioner. She now works as a freelance journalist, and has made numerous television and radio show appearances including: *The Glenn Beck Show, America Live* with Megyn Kelly, CNN's *Right on the Edge, Hannity's America, The O'Reilly Factor, The Mike Gallagher Show, Dennis Miller Radio, Sundays* with Eric Shawn and *The Red Eye* with Greg Gutfeld.

My dad is most definitely an interesting man to have as a father. He is as much a child at heart as he is a serious man of God, and that combination has made being his offspring an adventurous experience. You may not hear too many children say this about their parents, but I am actually glad my dad raised me the way he did; if I wasn't raised the way I was, I would probably be as bland as white rice. Just imagine being trapped on an island with only white rice to eat for the rest of your life. The thought alone is maddening.

Here are the spices my dad has added to my life that has made growing up in his casa very interesting:

1. He taught me to fear God and not men, which has forged me into a leader and not a lemming.

2. He taught me how to live life to the fullest and yet not get eaten alive by the world—which is nice because I have heard being eaten alive isn't a very pleasant experience.

3. He also afforded me the ability to protect myself with a strong B.S. detector, a few guns, throwing knives, and a spear (and he paid for self-defense classes at Valente Brothers Jiu-Jitsu).

These ingredients, though each very different, but equally essential, combined together to provide me with a life that I haven't gotten sick of. Raising a child is the single most important job any parent has. It's your legacy, your name, and your society's future that you are bringing up: HANDLE WITH CARE! Study this book to learn how to raise your daughter to be a righteous and rowdy girl.

Regis Giles

Regis Giles is a college student, Second Amendment Activist, the owner/creator of GirlsJustWannaHaveGuns.com and a contributing writer for NRA's magazine *InSights*. She is currently working on her hunting show, *Primal Urge*, which will be airing on the Pursuit Channel in the very near future. In addition, Regis has appeared on CNN's *Parker/Spitzer Show* and has been a speaker at CPAC the Nation's largest conservative gathering.

About the Author

Doug Giles is the creator and host of ClashRadio.com (IRN/USA Radio Network). In addition, Doug is a popular Columnist on Townhall.com, read moreminister, artist, Campus Lecturer and Author.

His articles have also appeared on several other print and online news sources, including *The Washington Times*, *New York Times*, *BigGovernment.com*, *USA Today*, *The Wall Street Journal*, *The Washington Examiner*, *NRA News*, *American Hunter* and *ABC News*. He has been a guest on both major television news programs and nationally syndicated radio shows across the nation.

Doug earned his Bachelor of Fine Arts degree from Texas Tech University and studied for his Master of Arts in Christianity and Culture from Knox Theological Seminary.

Doug and his wife Mary Margaret have two daughters: Hannah Giles who devastated ACORN with her undercover videos and Regis Giles who is a NRA columnist and 2nd Amendment activist. Giles' interests include guns, big game hunting, big game fishing, fine art, cigars and being a big pain in the butt to people who dislike God and the USA.

Other books by Doug Giles

Ruling in Babylon: Seven Habits of Highly Effective Twentysomethings (2003)

Political Twerps, Cultural Jerks, Church Quirks (2004)

The Bulldog Attitude: Get It or Get Left Behind (2006)

10 Habits of Decidedly Defective People: The Successful Loser's Guide to Life (2007)

A Time to Clash: Papers from a Provocative Pastor (2008)

If You're Going Through Hell Keep on Going (2009)

All Doug's books can be purchased at www.clashradio.com